Praise for *Bu*

Building Strong Writers is a feat of effective writing instruction strategies and solid rationale! As a former English teacher and current college professor, I recommend this book for anyone looking to teach the writing process effectively and efficiently. The models, examples, and organization make this book one you'll read and reference throughout your career!

—**Jenna Copper,** PhD, professor of education and coauthor of *Keeping the Wonder: An Educator's Guide to Magical, Engaging, and Joyful Learning*

Full of helpful sentence frames and step-by-step lesson plans, Christina has provided the tools to build strong writers! Her clear, easy-to-follow scaffolds ensure every educator can confidently guide their students through the writing process as they work to become proficient, skilled writers!

—**Ashley Bible,** coauthor of *Keeping the Wonder*

From its practical "teacher tips" to tried-and-true strategies and step-by-step guides, *Building Strong Writers* is a handbook for any ELA teacher who has ever been overwhelmed with teaching writing. After all, no matter how much you love to write, teaching it to today's teens is still tough. In this book, Christina breaks down the challenging task of writing into manageable chunks—for both students and teachers. Whether you're struggling with where to start, how to scaffold, or what to actually teach during your next writing unit, *Building Strong Writers* offers actionable ideas that you can read about today and implement tomorrow.

—**Abby Gross,** middle and high school ELA teacher and coauthor of *Keeping the Wonder*

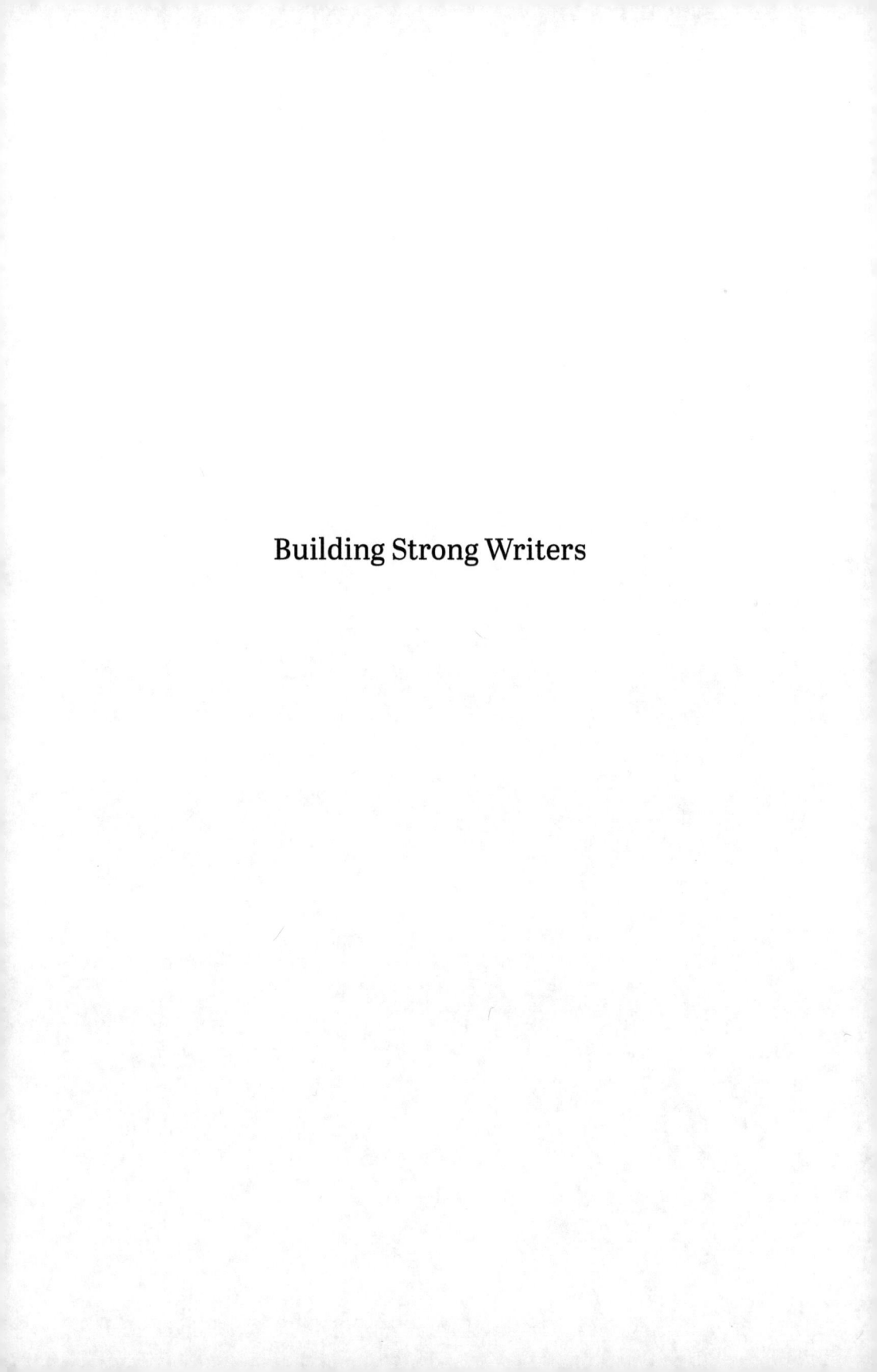

Building Strong Writers

Building Strong Writers

Strategies and Scaffolds
for Teaching Writing in Secondary ELA

Christina Schneider

Building Strong Writers: Strategies and Scaffolds for Teaching Writing in Secondary ELA
© 2024 Christina Schneider

All rights reserved. No part of this publication may be reproduced in any form or by any electronic or mechanical means, including information storage and retrieval systems, without permission in writing by the publisher, except by a reviewer who may quote brief passages in a review. For information regarding permission, contact the publisher at books@daveburgessconsulting.com.

> This book is available at special discounts when purchased in quantity for educational purposes or for use as premiums, promotions, or fundraisers. For inquiries and details, contact the publisher at books@daveburgessconsulting.com.

Published by Dave Burgess Consulting, Inc.
San Diego, CA
DaveBurgessConsulting.com

Library of Congress Control Number: 2024941201
Paperback ISBN: 978-1-956306-85-9
Ebook ISBN: 978-1-956306-86-6

Cover and interior design by Liz Schreiter
Edited and produced by Reading List Editorial
ReadingListEditorial.com

For all past, present, and future teachers, who help students reach their full potential; for my husband, who always believes in and supports me; for my children, who inspire me to be a better person, mother, and teacher.

Contents

1	Introduction: The Revolution Will Be Written
14	Chapter 1: Strategies
34	Chapter 2: Planning Backward
51	Chapter 3: Brainstorming
84	Chapter 4: Outlines
93	Chapter 5: The Three-Sentence Approach
100	Chapter 6: Reading Responses
115	Chapter 7: Collaborative Writing
123	Chapter 8: Your First Formal Writing Unit
137	Chapter 9: Peer Editing
146	Chapter 10: The First Five Minutes of Class
153	Chapter 11: Empowering Strong Writers
157	Acknowledgments
159	About the Author
160	References
162	More from Dave Burgess Consulting, Inc.

INTRODUCTION

The Revolution Will Be Written

The Irony of Writing Education

Teaching writing is challenging. And chances are, since you are either an English teacher or pursuing a career in teaching English Language Arts (ELA), the act of writing might come easily for you. I mean, English teachers do love words. However, being a good writer and a good writing teacher could not be more different. Being able to write well naturally does not necessarily translate to being able to teach writing effectively. But if we are going to teach our students to become stronger writers, then we also need to make sure our ELA classes meet the needs of every single one of our students. We need to purposefully include strategies and scaffolds in our instruction for the students who struggle with writing, the ones for whom writing does not come easily.

In my early years as an ELA teacher, I learned this irony firsthand. I've always loved expressing myself with words. Some of my earliest memories of writing go back to second grade when my elementary school had an in-house book publishing project. I remember my teacher, Mrs. Brown, and being so excited for an opportunity to publish my very own book, complete with my words, my illustrations, and fancy-schmancy black coil binding—all as a second grader. While I don't exactly remember what my book was about (I faintly remember a story about a girl and a well), I remember the love, passion, and excitement I felt toward writing. That was when I first realized how much I enjoyed writing.

A couple of years later, I vividly remember being in the fourth grade and furtively writing stories during math lessons. (Sorry, Mrs. Givens.) I was the author, and my friend Tomi was the illustrator. I looked forward to school each day because it meant time to be creative and imaginative as I poured my heart and soul into my stories. I escaped into my writing; it gave me a safe space and a creative outlet.

My love of writing extended beyond the four walls of my childhood classrooms. I fondly remember slumber parties at my cousin's house, where we would stay up late at night writing and creating a newspaper to deliver to my aunt and uncle the following day. We would write stories about what was happening in our lives, provide a weather forecast, and even tattle on our younger brothers and the shenanigans they were up to. We drew our newspaper layout, illustrated a comic section, and rolled up our homemade newspaper to deliver to my aunt and uncle's bedroom door in the morning. Unsurprisingly, I also advise the school's journalism program while teaching high school English!

My love for writing continued as I entered high school. I signed up for journalism (no shocker there) as an eager first-year student, and ever since then, I always knew I wanted to make writing a part of my life. On top of taking journalism all four years, I also served as my school's editor-in-chief. I interned at the local newspaper, where professional journalists mentored and helped me publish several stories in the *Las Vegas Review-Journal.*

That recognition led me to join "R-Jeneration," the high school intern program for the *LVRJ*. Even though my initial assignments for R-Jeneration—including an interview with up-and-coming NASCAR driver Kyle Busch—were terrifying, they were also exhilarating! In fact, my time as a reporter-in-training completely solidified my love of writing. I studied and majored in journalism in college, eventually becoming a high school English and journalism teacher.

Throughout my own educational and professional journey, writing has remained an essential part of my life. One of the most rewarding aspects of being a high school English teacher is helping students unlock their full potential and grow as writers. I remember the joy and exhilaration that writing brought me as a child and teenager, and now it is my mission to bring that same joy to all my students. Every student has the potential to be a great writer and embrace writing, but we must unlock that potential. Helping build students into strong, confident writers fills me with joy and keeps me going when teaching gets difficult.

But even as I've grown in skill as both a writer *and* a teacher, teaching writing has never become easy. As the years pass, I've noticed that students seem to struggle more and more with writing. From starting an essay to creative writing to forming thoughts into words, the art of writing seems to be more challenging for today's youth.

However, just because students don't know what to write doesn't mean they have nothing to say. In fact, that could not be further from the truth. Our students have so much to say; they are even bursting at the seams with ideas, but sometimes they might not know how to put their thoughts onto paper. These students have a story to tell. They have strong opinions and beliefs about the information they are writing, but writing might not be one of their natural strengths. So their brilliant ideas might never be shared in an ELA class or within a standard writing assignment. Sometimes, they need some guidance and assistance in structuring their words and thoughts.

If you are an older millennial like me, you might remember only a little writing instruction in your high school English classrooms growing up. I remember my teachers scrolling endlessly through their transparency notes as I desperately tried to copy everything verbatim before the teacher scrolled the transparency film into a roll, never to be seen again. I remember being so caught up in being able to write down the information and not miss a single sentence that I don't really remember practicing what we were supposed to do.

Most essays were assigned to be completed strictly outside the classroom. A typical scenario included going to school on Monday, being assigned an essay within the last five minutes of class, and having it be due at the start of class that Friday. Besides that, there wasn't any other mention of our essays until they were graded, marked up, and passed back. We would review a student's exemplary essay that the teacher had converted to a transparency sheet. In fact, looking back, most of our explicit writing instruction seemed to happen after the assignment.

Classroom instruction and best practices have changed immensely since the eighties and nineties, and now research shows that focused, specific, guided instruction, followed by the gradual release method, helps students retain information. That is where I base a lot of my writing instruction.

Ultimately, our role as ELA educators is not just to give students writing assignments and essays but also to provide students with the structure needed to succeed on those assignments. In that light, this book is for all students who struggle with writing and for all their teachers who want to equip them with all the tools necessary to be strong, confident writers. This book is for teachers who are trying their best to help their students become stronger writers. This book aims to create a shift in mindset around writing that will ultimately start a writing revolution. But what will that revolution look like?

I want to help you build strong, confident writers in your classroom. I want your students to look forward to their writing assignments because they know they have the skills, the know-how, and the ability to complete them well. I want students to rejoice in the art of composition. Rather than watching students struggle and even act out because writing is so intimidating, I want students to understand and capture the wondrous possibilities of effective writing. I want students to look forward to writing, to be confident in their writing, and to understand the power of the written word.

I want students to see that writing is so much more than an English assignment and that there are different kinds of writing with their own unique purposes. I want students to gain an inherent understanding that writing can give them the power to persuade people, inspire people, entertain people, and inform people. I want students to see that, through writing, they can look back on their learning and reflect on the vast world around them. I want students to view writing as a valuable and necessary tool that will prepare them for their futures.

Building (and Scaffolding) on Failure

My vision of a revolution in student writing had humble beginnings. I remember my very first teaching assignment like it was yesterday. I was young, still in my preservice teaching program, and desperately trying to teach a group of students I did not know how to reach. I was given a long-term substitute teaching assignment in a ninth-grade remediation class where all students were below grade level, and most were second language learners. I was a long-term substitute without my full teaching credential coming into their classroom when their teacher unexpectedly left early. I was in over my head, but I didn't even know it.

To be honest, I failed those students miserably, which I haven't let go of in more than a decade in the classroom. I didn't understand where my students were and what they needed.

For the most part, the experience was a classroom management nightmare. For weeks, we all struggled together. I would review lessons, go over readings, and give a writing assignment the students wouldn't do. Our classroom culture deteriorated in all my students' attempts not to work on assignments, and eventually, they acted out.

The start of every class period was the same. My students were going from the chaos of the passing period to immediate instruction. The bell would ring, and the students would be all over the place. They weren't in their assigned seats. They hung out and conversed at the door. They were on the classroom furniture, and when I asked them to sit in their seats, my students completely ignored me.

I would try to get my students ready to start class, but things didn't work, so I would raise my voice and yell in a desperate attempt to begin class. I actually tried to start class like that. After about fifteen minutes, my students would eventually calm down, but then they would fire spit wads and hold side conversations as I attempted direct instruction. It was a nightmare.

My failures weren't just around classroom management but more about instructional design. I naively walked into the room and assumed that writing a paragraph about a brief nonfiction passage in a ninth-grade English class would be easy for my students. It *wasn't* an easy task for this class, but I missed all the red flags. I just assumed my students were acting up because it was a challenging or even a "bad" group of kids. I was too quick to think that all of the tension and frustration in the classroom was because of the students' poor behavior and not my inadequate teaching practices.

When a group of students flat-out refused to take out a piece of paper and write the paragraph, I assumed they were being defiant because they weren't following instructions. I didn't even consider that they were refusing to participate out of self-preservation because they didn't have the language to write the requested paragraph. When a kid would get out of their seat, walk around, and mess with other students, I thought they did so because they were trying to be disrespectful. I didn't view it as a way to avoid doing the assignment out of fear of failure.

My presumptions about these groups of students and their abilities could not be further from the truth. Looking back, I would have had more success had I known more about creating a positive classroom culture and developing meaningful relationships in the classroom. However, I also needed to know exactly where my students were. I needed to understand their abilities, strengths, and weaknesses.

It took me weeks to realize why these students acted this way: I did not provide them with the support and scaffolding they needed to feel confident enough in their writing abilities to complete assignments. I went into the classroom assuming students had the skills they needed, without meeting them where they were. As I said, I failed them during those first few weeks.

At that time, though, I didn't even know I was failing my students; I couldn't see past my frustrations. Since writing always came naturally and organically to me, I assumed the same would be true for my students. I was so wrong. I mistook my students' acting out as bad behavior rather than a way for them to express that they didn't understand my lessons. And even worse, I mistook their poor writing for a lack of effort.

I wish I could take back our weeks and weeks of struggling together. I wish I knew back then what I know now. I wish I could go back and spend time with those students all over again. However, we sometimes learn our most valuable lessons from our biggest failures. I wish learning how to become a stronger educator didn't come from failed experiences, but those failed experiences cause us to reflect and grow.

It wasn't until one day, when I haphazardly wrote some sentence frames on the whiteboard, that I was finally able to meet my first students at their level and help them complete their work. As many people do, I naively thought I was completing the assignment for them by writing a brief fill-in-the-blank paragraph on the wall, but it worked. After our class reading, every single student sat at their desk and wrote. They were all engaged in the assignment. This change in my approach and my students' behavior led me to a significant epiphany that changed how I approached instruction in the classroom, as well as my attitude toward the kids.

Everything changed once I could assess my students' needs and meet them at their academic level. Most classroom management issues I was experiencing went away; my students were able to learn and demonstrate their understanding. It actually felt like I was teaching the students rather than just asking them to sit at their assigned seats and stop talking as I attempted to go over the lesson for the day.

By meeting my students where they were, the entire dynamic of the classroom changed. This change did not happen overnight but gradually as the students became more comfortable in class. Rather than coming into the classroom worried about an assignment that was far beyond their grasp, they gradually saw that they were capable of completing the work in the classroom. They began to trust the process of learning, engaging, and trying in our classroom, but more importantly, they began to trust me as their teacher.

That one lightbulb moment, that one day when I haphazardly wrote some sentence stems on the whiteboard in my early teaching career, left an unforgettable impression on me as an educator. Ever since then, I have approached every single class period and school year with the idea that my students may or may not be able to complete grade-level work and assignments and show mastery similar to previous classes. Every single new class period and year is an opportunity for me as an educator to assess where my new students are and meet their needs.

And this transformation with my first class is what really illustrates the difference between being a good writer and a good writing teacher: patience and understanding. I needed to have patience with my students as they practiced essential skills. I needed to learn how to help my students become stronger writers. I needed to learn how to help them organize and convey their thoughts. I had to push through my own understanding of what I thought a ninth grader should be able to do (and also push through the common core standards of what a ninth grader should be able to do) and reach my students at their level. I needed to develop a structured and scaffolded approach to writing instruction.

Providing structured and scaffolded writing instruction is not about doing the challenging work for our students or writing their assignments for them. Structured and scaffolded writing instruction is not about giving students the answers. Instead, it shows students how to write academically and how to organize their thoughts carefully. Structured and scaffolded writing instruction meets students where they need you and delivers personalized instruction to help them grow and flourish as writers. Structured and scaffolded instruction helps students learn, focus on, and practice the skills you are teaching—without overwhelming them and making them waste brain power and energy on a more advanced skill you *aren't* currently teaching.

How to Use This Book

If you are reading this book, you are ready to dive into more engaging and effective writing instruction. And that means that you are also prepared to start planning for a writing revolution in your own classroom.

My teaching philosophy starts from scratch and builds up strong writers one skill at a time by breaking down challenging writing instruction into easy-to-manage, accessible chunks of information. Writing, as it is, is already a tedious and seemingly insurmountable skill, and teaching writing and delivering effective writing instruction is even more difficult. This book is organized in a way that does just that: it breaks down the process of writing instruction so teachers are better equipped with the skills and strategies they need to meet their students at their current ability levels.

Every chapter within this book is meant to inspire you to meet your students where they are, provide fun and engaging writing instruction within your classroom, and empower you to be the most effective ELA teacher you can be. Each chapter will provide you with invaluable tools, strategies, and classroom exercises you can incorporate with the lessons and units you already teach to help you become a more effective writing teacher for your students.

I strategically chose to include some of my favorite writing strategies in this book—those that are tried and true and deliver results. Each chapter of this book strategically builds on complexity, while also following the natural progression of the writing process so you can use this book as a writing tool from the beginning of the school year to the end. Furthermore, I discuss "activities" and "strategies" throughout this book. The activities you read about are classroom activities and exercises you can do with your students as you are teaching them writing. The strategies are different educational approaches you incorporate alongside your instruction to help students become stronger writers.

There are a couple of ways to use this book. The first would be to read it all the way through as you mark it up with your own ideas, annotations, and draft lesson plans. This approach is beneficial if you are reading it as professional development over the summer or toward the beginning of the school year. You'll be able to take and use the content of this book in your classroom from day one. The other would be to read select chapters of this book as you plan your writing instruction and find what best fits your current assignment. This approach will work best if you are reading this book during the middle of the school year or as you are currently working through a writing unit with your students. You'll be able to tailor content from this book to use in your classroom right where you are in the school year. Whatever your approach, this book contains engaging and effective strategies and activities you can read about and apply in your classroom.

This book is meant to be modular. For example, if you are assigning an essay in your classroom, perhaps you'll want to select one of the brainstorming activities from chapter 3 to include in your instruction before your students start drafting their essays. Or maybe your students have already drafted their essays, and you are looking for exciting ways to engage your learners in peer or self-editing. In that case, turn to chapter 9. I hope that by reading this book and implementing the content and ideas this way, you will become a more effective writing teacher and feel inspired to implement more strategies and scaffolds into your current writing instruction.

Important Markers

Throughout this book, for each activity or strategy you'll notice four indicators designed to organize content so you can more easily and practically implement the strategies and ideas found in this book.

DAILY LEARNING OBJECTIVE: This is the Daily Learning Objective. Many districts and schools require teachers to include DLOs in daily lesson plans and prominently display them on the board for students. Pedagogical research affirms the value of posting DLOs. Posting and communicating daily learning objectives for students helps improve their motivation and achievement. Furthermore, DLOs also help teachers communicate learning goals with their students (Althoff et al. 2007, 43–58). I've included sample DLOs with each student activity and teaching strategy in this book. These DLOs are written in student-friendly language to help teachers and students measure student learning.

> **Teacher Tip:** While I filled this book with activities and strategies you can implement in the classroom, no two classes are ever the same. In every class period a teacher leads, they will experience unique challenges. I designed the Teacher Tip sections throughout the book to provide teachers with varied ways to include these strategies in light of students' specific needs. Teacher Tips offer practical advice with experience-based ideas and lessons.

STUDENT CHALLENGE: Just as every class period is different, every student in that class period is also different. Some students are ready for a challenge: they have demonstrated their understanding of the basics and have an innate hunger to improve their writing skills and challenge themselves in the classroom. Student Challenges meet the needs of those students in many of my writing lessons, especially as we progress through the school year. Whenever I communicate a Student Challenge with the class, I ensure my students know two things. First, I inform all my students of my expectations for the lesson. Second,

I invite every student in the class who wants to grow as a writer to attempt the Student Challenge. Some students will eagerly accept the Student Challenge, struggle through the work necessary to accomplish it, and become stronger writers as a result, while others might shy away. The important thing, however, is that even if students do not attempt the challenge, they still know and meet the lesson expectations. By inviting and encouraging all of my students to try the challenge, I offer differentiated instruction while inclusively modeling higher-level learning for all of my students.

> **Action Step:** These organizers and step-by-step guides are built to help you plan each activity for your class.

Regardless of where you are in the school year, this book provides the tools, strategies, and flexibility you need to improve your writing instruction and teach your students how to become stronger writers. Reach for this book if you have a couple of extra days during your writing unit and want to add in some direct instruction and strategies for what your students are currently working on. Or reach for this book as you plan out your first formal writing assignment and use it as a unit-long or even yearlong guide to help you implement and deliver effective writing instruction, lessons, and activities. Either way, regardless of where you are in the school year, this book provides you with guidance, pacing, and on-the-fly strategies.

In Summary

The strategies, tools, and action steps I provide in this book will help you become more confident in teaching writing to your students, and it will help you give your students the tools they need to become stronger writers. Whether you read this book from start to finish and plan out your school year alongside your reading, or if you refer to a specific chapter as needed for strategies and ideas throughout the school year, this book covers the entire writing process, including actionable classroom activities and strategies.

My goal for this book is for it to be one of your companions throughout the school year—a guide you turn to when you notice your students might need a little more support with their writing.

For you as a teacher, I hope the content, ideas, and strategies here empower you to improve your instruction, make you feel confident about trying new classroom strategies, and inspire you to fall in love with teaching preteens and teenagers to write. I also hope it helps affirm that teaching writing is a monumental task, but our best success will come when we slow down and take it one step at a time.

For your school community, I hope you take the strategies in this book, share them with your colleagues, and implement them in multiple classrooms—helping so many students gain the skills and confidence they need to become strong writers. As a teacher, I've found that some of my most impactful growth happens when I sit down with my colleagues and discuss what is working and what isn't. I hope the content in this book can help you discuss what instructional strategies your students need.

For your students, especially those who come into your classroom intimidated by the daunting task of writing, I hope these strategies will give them the confidence to know they can write and aren't as bad as they think they are at writing. I also want your students to feel empowered to be the strongest writers they can be.

CHAPTER 1

Strategies

When I started teaching high school English, like so many other first-year and new teachers, I felt like I was starting from scratch. I had to learn a new curriculum. I had to write or review assessments and writing assignments. I also had to develop effective instruction and activities that would prepare my students to meet learning objectives. In those first few years, it was a lot.

Looking back, I did a lot of research on *how* to set up my lessons and *how* to structure my classroom activities for effective learning. Throughout this process, I learned through trial and error. Everything seemed to work on paper, and in my mind, I truly believed my lessons would succeed; however, they were often not as successful as I thought they would be. A few activities were downright failures, and I jumped ship and shifted gears in the middle of a class period. On the other hand, there have also been plenty of times when I haphazardly put something together at the last minute, and I didn't think it would be that effective, but it worked.

While trial and error inevitably seems to be an integral part of teaching, I can tell you this: each year in the classroom, I've grown more confident in my teaching style and teacher tool kit. A teacher tool kit is an exhaustive list of winning, effective, and go-to strategies that work year after year. Frequently, these strategies are best practices, or derivatives of best practices, that have been used by educators for decades, and there is a reason for their longevity. Research-based teaching strategies are proven. They are practical, and they work.

While pedagogy is always evolving and shifting, these effective, engaging, and practical strategies work. To kick off the body section of this book, I want to introduce what I call my six major "strategies": quick-and-easy, high-impact practices that can be folded into everyday activities whenever I find myself with five or ten extra minutes in a course period. These strategies build strong writers by giving students a solid foundation of necessary writing skills, showing students what exemplary writing looks like, and assisting students with their academic writing on their way to becoming stronger writers.

Mentor Texts

A mentor text is any text—ranging from a whole novel, to a passage, to an essay, to an excerpt—that models what good writers do well to a student audience. Mentor texts work off of the idea that we learn new skills through imitation; we look for examples to follow and emulate (Gallagher 2014).

Mentor texts are one of my favorite strategies to use in the classroom because they serve as an exemplary writing model for students who might not have had much exposure to a broad range of writing types, styles, and techniques. Effective mentor texts can be any length—ranging from just a single sentence to an entire book—so they are ideal to use during instruction because you can use them in one class period for a single lesson or use them over a prolonged period encompassing an entire unit. Mentor texts help students see, read, and internalize what effective writing is, and they also provide students with a model for which to strive.

Effectively using mentor texts in the classroom requires more than simply sharing a text with the students. To really maximize the benefit of mentor texts, it is important to think aloud with your students as you read and review a text in class. As you read together, point out specific sentences, or portions of sentences, and describe what the author did well and explain why it is so effective.

How to use mentor texts

1. Identify the passage you would like to use with your students.
2. Provide the passage to all your students. This will ensure all students can read the passage, understand it, and use it as a mentor text.
3. Prompt students to engage with the text. Have them read the text on their own first. Then, let them know that you think the author did something particularly well in the passage. Either have students work in partners or small groups to read and analyze the text and try to identify that quality.
4. Identify the essential parts of the mentor text and explain what you believe the author did well. Have students highlight these essential parts on their own copies of the text.
5. If possible, and this step is very beneficial, provide additional examples of writing tactics that work particularly well in the mentor text.
6. Charge students with the task of writing using the mentor text as an example.

Finding mentor texts doesn't have to be a long, arduous process. I recommend keeping a pen and a pack of small sticky notes handy whenever you read, even when you read for pleasure. If you notice the author using a semicolon in a particularly effective way, or if you notice that the author included vivid descriptive language or used another writing technique particularly well, make a quick note in the book and on the sticky note and move on.

One of my absolutely favorite mentor texts is an excerpt from Jason Reynolds's verse novel *Long Way Down*. I like to use the poem "BEEF"

Strategies

as a mentor text because it is short but packs a punch with its elaborate use of the extended simile. When I present this text to my students, I do so with the goal of teaching them about the extended simile and how an author can carry a comparison through multiple lines of text to enhance its meaning.

Here is how I did this in my classroom with Jason Reynolds's poem "BEEF."

1. As I read the book for the first time before teaching it, this poem stood out to me immediately. From my previous teaching experience, I knew that high school students struggle with extended similes. They get a simile. They can write and identify a simple simile. However, the extended simile is challenging and requires additional higher-level thinking. Immediately, I knew this poem was special and that I would want to use it in the classroom as a mentor text. I dog-eared the page the poem was printed on and kept reading, knowing I would revisit that poem.
2. All of my students had a class copy of the text, but that book was a school library book, and my students couldn't mark up the text. In addition to the class set of books, I typed up the poem into a document and shared that with my students digitally.
3. Initially, we listened to the poem in class as part of our class reading. I didn't stop the audio and point anything out; I simply let my students enjoy the story. However, I went back to that poem toward the end of the class period once we were done with the reading for the day. I had all of my students turn to that page, and we closely read that poem again. I told my students that Jason Reynolds did something particularly effective here with figurative language, and I asked my students to partner up and try to identify what it was. Most

students identified the use of his simile, but most did not catch on to the extended part of the simile.
4. Once students had time to explore the text without my help, I stepped in and explained what an extended simile is; I pointed out the extended simile, highlighted various portions of the text, and had my students highlight their text.
5. Since there is only one poem in the book like this, I wrote my own using Reynolds's poem "BEEF" as a mentor text. I shared my original poem with my students and had them identify the same key elements from Reynolds's poem in my poem.
6. Finally, I tasked the kids with a fun and creative assignment. Using any school-appropriate topic of their choice, they were to model Reynolds's writing and write their own poem using an extended simile.

However, mentor passages work well with more than just poems; they work with all types of writing. When I introduce mentor texts in the classroom, I keep the passages relatively short, preferably a single side of a piece of paper, and I provide paper copies to each student. This ensures that my students can read mentor texts directly and actively engage with the text, annotate, and take notes. I want my students to write notes in the margins about what they are thinking so they can pinpoint a specific strategy or technique from the mentor text, make a note of it, learn how to employ it in their own writing, and then master the skill. I want them to highlight and underline specific techniques authors employ. I want them to be completely immersed in the text. The more exposure they have to a broad range of exemplary writing and the more they actively interact with high-quality mentor texts, the more likely students will be to duplicate the skills, styles, and strategies in their own writing.

That said, using mentor texts in the classroom only goes so far if the mentor text is a stand-alone strategy. When using mentor texts, especially when teaching writing, teachers will have the most success when they also employ additional strategies. Yes, seeing an example sentence or paragraph is helpful for students learning how to write. However, if they don't understand each part of the text, if they don't break it down and understand what each element is and why it is essential, students will have a hard time transferring that information from the mentor text to their own writing and having a modeled writing skill stick. That is why using multiple strategies alongside each other is so important, especially toward the beginning of the school year.

Color-Coding

When students type into a word processing application or write with a pencil on a paper, all of the words look the same. They are formatted the same in the same color, so nothing in particular stands out, and students do not need to switch colors or change the font color to highlight an important element of a sentence. This is why, as a strategy, color-coding is so important in the ELA classroom. Having students color-code their written responses helps them slow down and focus on the actual impact and intentionality of every single word and phrase. While color-coding elements with their essays might take longer, it shows that students know what they are doing, and it exemplifies their responses.

One of the best things about using color-coding as a strategy is that there are so many ways to implement it in the classroom. I use color-coding for everything from helping my students organize their essays to writing a solid thesis statement to learning how to embed quotes properly in their writing. On top of color-coding being beneficial for the students, it also helps make grading faster and simpler. It's a win-win.

Using color-coding as an instructional strategy helps increase engagement in writing instruction and helps students learn how to organize their work better (Geigle 2014).

By color-coding a sentence, students are more likely to tackle that sentence one piece at a time. Adding in the color-coding strategy as students examine their own writing also helps students break down their sentences, which provides an additional opportunity for self-editing: as students go back to color-code their sentences, they will read the sentence, analyze it to see which color they need to use, and, ideally, make edits if needed. Getting students to a point where they can write a similar sentence takes time and practice. Color-coding the sentence, breaking it down, and identifying each part really helps students learn how to write academically.

The first time I used color-coding in my high school English class was when I taught my students how to properly embed and cite a quote in their writing. I usually start teaching this skill during the second week of school, but I focus on it all year. My students' first academic writing assignment is a literary analysis response that is only three sentences long.

> You can read more about this first writing response, which includes a topic sentence, quote sentence, and explanation sentence, in chapter 5, which covers the three-sentence response format.

Color-coding a quote sentence

When I use color-coding to teach my students how to embed a quote in their writing, there are four areas I focus on: indicator, lead-in, quote, and citation. For each of those elements, I use a different color. I may draw the embedded quote from a mentor sentence or use sentence frames as well. For the sake of black-and-white printing, I will show what color-coding might look like using <u>underlined</u>, **bolded**, plain, and *italicized* text. As you review the information in this section, please feel free to practice what we do in the classroom: engage with the text! Use colorful pens or highlighters to distinguish each part of the example sentences and accompanying explanation so you can truly see how powerful color-coding in the ELA classroom can be.

Example sentence

<u>For example,</u> **after Josephine learns of her husband's death, she realizes,** "There would be no one to live for her during those coming years; she would live for herself" *(Chopin).*

As they write or type, I have students underline each part of the sentence with the designated color if they are writing by hand or change the font color on their document if they are typing. Here, I broke down the sentence containing the contextual evidence into four parts: the <u>academic transition,</u> **the context leading into the quote,** the quote, and *the citation.*

Getting students to a place academically where they are able to write a similar sentence and embed their evidence seamlessly into their sentence takes a lot of time, practice, and repetition. Color-coding the sentence, breaking it down, and identifying each part helps students learn how to write academically because it focuses their attention on each required part of the sentence.

By color-coding the sentence, students are more likely to tackle the sentence one piece at a time. Adding in the color-coding elements helps students break down the sentence, and it also provides an additional aspect of self-editing because as students go back to color-code their sentences, they will read the sentence, analyze it to see which color they need to use, and, ideally, make edits if needed.

Color-coding a thesis statement

Once students progress to multiparagraph responses, I teach them how to write a basic, functioning thesis statement. Once students can demonstrate that they know how to write a more formulaic thesis statement, I have them start playing around with their writing style. However, I first like to see that they understand the fundamentals.

I explain to my students that a thesis statement is like a road map or a blueprint for their essay. It should contain all of the big-picture information that the essay will go on to explain. A thesis statement should include two key elements: it should answer the essay prompt and briefly state the supporting reasons.

By color-coding the thesis statement, we help our students respond to the prompt, stay on topic, and set up their essays logically. Before getting to this point in the writing process, however, I like to have my students participate in some form of collaborative essay brainstorming activity to have an idea about what they want to write about. If students have some ideas about what they want to write about, they will have an easier time writing their thesis statement.

Example thesis statement

<u>One of the most essential inventions affecting people's everyday lives is the traffic light,</u> which *helps control traffic flow* and **increases safety**.

Using color-coding to teach students how to write a basic thesis statement, you'll instruct students to underline the portion of the thesis statement that best answers the prompt and then use a different color for each supporting reason. In the example above, I underlined the part of the thesis statement that answers the prompt and then used italics and bold text to showcase the two supporting reasons. For argument writing, I also encourage students to assign an additional color to acknowledge the opposing viewpoint in the thesis statement.

From this example thesis statement, the writing prompt for this writing assignment is probably about an important invention that affects society. From there, you can infer that the student chose the traffic light because of how traffic lights help traffic flow better and help keep people safe by reducing collisions.

Color-coding for essay organization

Implementing a successful color-coding strategy does not have to stop at one sentence. You can carry color-coding throughout an entire essay to help students stay on topic and organize their writing cohesively. Let's continue with the thesis statement example from above and see how this would play out in a student draft.

In the draft essay, have students highlight the thesis statements and then write or type each of their topic sentences in the designated color they chose in the same order of ideas in their thesis statements. By highlighting their thesis statements, students show you they know which sentence is their thesis statement and where it should be placed in the essay.

Thesis statement	One of the most essential inventions affecting people's everyday lives is the traffic light, which helps control traffic flow and increases safety.
Body paragraph one topic sentence	*This topic sentence should be written in one color, whichever color you or the student chooses, but it should be the first supporting reason listed in the thesis statement as indicated in this book by the italicized text, and it should be about how traffic lights help control the flow of traffic.* To help students stay organized, remind them that everything in this paragraph needs to be related to their topic sentence. It needs to be about controlling and improving traffic flow.
Body paragraph two topic sentence	**This topic sentence should be written in a second color, whichever color you or the student chooses, but it should be the second supporting reason listed in the thesis statement as indicated in this book by the bolded text, and it should be about how traffic lights increase safety.** To help students stay organized, remind them that everything in this paragraph needs to be related to their topic sentence. It needs to be about increasing safety on the road.

Once students reach this point in their writing journey, they are ready to outline.

Sentence Frames

A sentence frame is a structured chunk of text with fill-in-the-blank spaces for students to add their own unique ideas and thoughts. There are many benefits of using sentence frames as a go-to strategy. One of the biggest benefits is that sentence frames boost student confidence and efficacy, especially in our ELA students. Because sentence frames help eliminate writer's block and provide students with a frame in which to formulate their ideas, they help students feel more confident about their writing, especially once they have a start to their response. Using sentence frames in the classroom also helps English learners develop stronger language skills, while also making academic vocabulary much more accessible (Donnelly and Row 2010, 133–134).

One common misconception about using sentence frames as part of formal writing instruction is that sentence frames "do the work for the students" or "dumb down" the writing process. This is simply not true. Rather, sentence frames teach students how to write, not what to write. While sentence frames provide a basic framework and organization for their writing, the students fill in the blanks with their own thoughts and analysis.

Example sentence frames

These sentence frames are prompt-specific. When using frames in the classroom, you will want to tailor the sentence frame you are providing to your students to match and completely answer the entire prompt.

Writing about Literature

Sample Prompt	Sample Sentence Frame	Potential Student Response
Write a paragraph about how the author uses descriptive language to develop the setting and conflict of the story.	In the short story "Title," author _____ [strong verb] _____ to _____. For example, [explain what is going on in the story to introduce the quote], "quote" (cite). [Author's name in possessive form] use of _____ enhances the story's setting because _____.	In the short story "The Veldt," author Ray Bradbury uses descriptive language to enhance the setting and conflict of the story to draw his audience in. For example, as the parents are investigating the trouble in the nursery, they saw, "the lions now, fifteen feet away, so real, so feverishly and startlingly real that you could feel the prickling fur on your hand, and your mouth was stuffed with the dusty upholstery smell of their heated pelts" (Bradbury). Bradbury's use of descriptive language enhances the story's setting of the nursery because he makes it seem so real that George and Lydia can actually taste and feel the veldt.
Write a paragraph about how the conflict first arises in *Lord of the Flies*.	In the novel _____ by _____, the conflict first arises when _____ and _____, which ultimately causes _____.	In the novel *Lord of the Flies*, the conflict first arises when Jack and Ralph hold a vote to determine who will be the leader of the island, which ultimately causes a large clash and a war between the two groups of children.

Writing about Nonfiction

Sample Prompt	Sample Sentence Frame	Potential Student Response
Write a paragraph that explains the author's main purpose of the passage.	In the essay entitled "_____," author _____'s main purpose is to _____.	In the essay "The Hidden Dangers of Consuming Too Much Sugar," author Christina Schneider's main purpose is to educate the audience about how consuming too much sugar is harmful to the human body.
Write a paragraph about the purpose of the speech.	_____, in his/her/their speech "_____," discusses how _____ and _____ work together to _____.	President Abraham Lincoln, in his speech "The Gettysburg Address," discusses how that nation should never forget the atrocities of the Civil War and should work together to ensure its longevity.

Sentence Starters

Sentence starters, or sentence stems, are another useful and effective tool for writing instruction in all grades. While this strategy is similar to the sentence frame, there is a key difference: sentence frames provide support throughout an entire paragraph; sentence starters are typically for just one sentence at a time. As I work my way through scaffolding writing in the classroom throughout the year, I like to gradually release the responsibility of writing an entire paragraph, and then an entire essay, to my students. However, I first begin with sentence frames. Once students are comfortable with that strategy, I then take away some of the structure and provide them with just sentence starters.

Using sentence starters in the classroom is a great way to help all learners grow and improve as writers. Even students in their senior year of high school benefit from sentence starters.

Sentence stems are a great way to help a student begin a higher-level conversation about the topic, either aloud or on paper.

Example sentence starters

To summarize a point made in the conversation or text

- This article is mainly about _____.
- In summary, _____.

To agree with a person or the author

- I agree with _____ because _____.
- _____'s argument that _____ is important because _____.
- I like what _____ added to the conversation because _____.

To disagree with a person or the author

- I disagree with _____ because _____.
- _____'s argument that _____ is incomplete because _____.
- While _____ said, _____, I think that _____.

To add to the conversation

- Building off what _____ said, I also think _____.
- To add to _____'s point about _____, I also want to say _____.
- In addition to _____, we should also think about _____.

Academic Language Word Banks

One of the final writing strategies I like to use with my students is Academic Language Word Banks. These Word Banks are similar to the Word Banks students might have seen in their younger elementary days, but they are more sophisticated now because the students are tackling more sophisticated writing prompts and learning more complex writing features.

One of the reasons many of our students prefer math to English is because in math, you have a definitive right or wrong answer. This isn't the case in English class. However, that is one of the beauties of the ELA class and the written and spoken word. There is more than just one way to arrive at your destination. Likewise, students experience success when they have a path or a formula to follow. Providing students with Academic Language Word Banks gives them the guidance and support they need to write well. By sharing Academic Language Word Banks with students, we are providing them with the essential academic language and style they need to be successful. Similar to how a mentor text shows students an example of exemplary writing, an Academic Language Word Bank shows them the direct path to exemplary writing.

> ### My mentor teacher helped build me into a stronger teacher
>
> One of the most helpful Academic Language Word Banks comes from my mentor teacher, Mrs. Kay Williams Pierce; I include this tool with her permission. As I mentioned before, teaching is my second career; I entered the world of teacher education programs and student teaching after I already had a full-time, salaried position in public relations. Despite my previous experience in public relations, entering the world of education was an entirely new beast. No matter how many teacher preparation classes you take, how many educational-based professional development books you read, and how many teacher-written blogs you read, videos you watch, or social media content you consume, nothing truly prepares you for what it will be like in the classroom. Student teaching helps prepare you, but the real learning happens in your classroom with your students in those first three or four years.

However, student teaching is the most authentic experience that helps prepare teacher candidates for life in the classroom, and to be completely honest, student teaching is somewhat awkward. You are welcomed into an established teacher's classroom where they already have their year started. The students are in a routine, are used to their teacher, and already understand how things work in that classroom. And because of those reasons, student teaching can be a daunting and intimidating challenge.

When I started my student teaching, I also had a unique obstacle: I was recovering from knee surgery. Before my student teaching started, I had revision ACL reconstructive surgery, and I was on crutches and in a full thigh-to-ankle knee brace. Recovery and physical therapy for a revision ACL surgery takes more time and care than standard ACL reconstructive surgery rehab. I didn't really have an option about this, either. I needed the surgery, but I was already scheduled to do my student teaching that spring. I couldn't delay my surgery, and if I postponed my student teaching, that would have set me back an entire semester in my teacher credential program and an entire school year for getting my first teaching job. So there I was: student teaching with my crutches and leg brace. I would awkwardly side-crutch through the classroom to make my way around and check on the students, and I would partially crumple papers I passed out to the students, holding the papers in my hand on the hand grips of the crutches. It really must have been a sight to see.

I completed my student teaching at the school where my in-laws worked. It is a school in my current district but not where I currently teach. I was placed part-time in Kay's classroom for most of the school day and in another teacher's classroom for a couple of class periods. Kay is a super-organized teacher with a wealth of knowledge and a natural teacher. I remember first observing her and watching her in the classroom as she carried herself with authority and compassion, and it was just the right amount of both. She was strict yet fair. Her students respected her, and they responded well to her lessons. She had bookshelves and cabinets filled with binders upon binders of immaculately organized lessons, teaching materials, novel units, reading quizzes, grammar worksheets, and so much more. Each page of teaching materials was carefully placed in a sheet protector and organized with binder tabs and labels. On top of how she carried herself in her classroom and how she organized her classroom, she seemed to know everything about teaching English. Her depth of content knowledge was truly astounding and downright intimidating. As a young student teacher, I would think, "How am I ever going to be able to do this?" However, the way she worked with her students, demonstrating compassion and patience and having a genuine desire to help them learn, was the same way she worked with me. Even though many times as a student teacher, I felt inadequate in trying to stand in her shoes, that is just the nature of student teaching and learning the art of becoming a teacher. It's a practice that takes years.

Ultimately, Kay moved to another school in the district, and I was finally hired at my current district eight years later—the same district where I completed my student teaching. Today, Kay and I teach at the same school. She is in the classroom across the hallway from me, and she still is that compassionate and knowledgeable mentor I had during my student teaching years. In addition to my department chair, Kay is one of the first people I turn to when I have a question, need advice, or want to talk something through. We even teach together on the same sophomore-level English team, and while it might be an insignificant coincidence to some people, I find great joy and comfort in knowing she is there and that her door is always open if I ever have a question.

Now for the Strategy

I tell this story about Kay and her wealth of knowledge because this next writing strategy comes from her. Before she shared this tool with me, I used all the strategies mentioned above to help teach my students how to correctly embed a quote in their writing. I was giving them sentence frames to use, and it was working. However, I noticed the sentence frames I used didn't work for every quote, making for some awkward evidence sentences. My instruction for embedding evidence was missing the indicator and the verb.

Building Concrete Detail Sentences

General Transition, + Contextual Lead-In (Set Up the Situation + Describe the Situation + Indicator + Verb) + "Quote" + (citation).

	\multicolumn{3}{c}{**CONTEXTUAL LEAD-IN**}			
General Transition,	**Set Up the Situation**	**Describe the Situation**	**Indicator** (who said the quote or did the action)	**Verb**	**"Quote"**	**(Citation)**
For example, For instance, In addition, Also, Second, Furthermore, Likewise, Finally,	when before because while during after even though since	a brief description of what is happening when the quote appears in the text	the author the narrator the writer character name author's last name he she they	claims says reveals explains observes believes states argues	Dialogue or text taken directly out of the text and placed in quotation marks	The page number where the quoted text can be found written inside of parenthesis without p., pp., pg., or page

Using this Academic Language Word Bank and adding those two elements made all the difference in my writing instruction as a high school English teacher. As a result, instead of students writing an awkward sentence beginning with "The quote says . . . " or "The story says . . . " or having an awkward run-on or fragment sentence with the quote, students wrote more fluidly. I found this strategy essential in helping students elevate their writing as they moved to high school from middle school. They embedded their evidence seamlessly where the transition from their own writing to the quote blends coherently and grammatically correctly.

How to Use Academic Language Word Banks

I typically introduce Academic Language Word Banks to my students toward the beginning of the school year, during our short story unit. We write about every short story we read in class, first starting with a three-sentence response, moving on to a four-sentence response, then a full-paragraph response, and finally with a complete, multiparagraph essay.

During one of our first writing assignments, I provide the Word Bank (below) to my students, and I tell them to hold on to it for the entire school year—and even to use it the following school year. Along with this Word Bank, I provide my students with two mentor sentences from the stories we previously read in class. These mentor sentences are important because, for this strategy to work, students need to be familiar with the stories to glean the evidence from so they can see how setting up and describing the situation truly works. Then, I have my students color-code every element in the Word Bank and then color-code the mentor sentences. Usually, the day before, we color-code one sentence together to introduce that strategy.

Here is what the Word Bank looks like when my students first receive it. If you scan the QR code, you'll see what the chart looks like once my students and I go through the color-coding exercise together. I instruct them to use highlighters or light-colored markers (both of which I have available for my students to use) as they complete this task. You'll also have access to a file of this chart and color photos!

I have my students use their color-coded Academic Language Word Bank with every writing assignment they use. Not only does this chart help students embed their quotes properly, but it also helps students learn how to do this. After using this chart several times, many students will be able to do this without needing to reference the chart.

Building Concrete Detail Sentences

General Transition, + Contextual Lead In (Set up the Situation + Describe the situation + Indicator + Verb) + "Quote" + (citation).

General Transition,	Set up the Situation	Describe the Situation	Indicator (who said the quote or did the action)	Verb	"Quote"	(citation)
For example,	when	A brief	the author	claims	Dialogue or	The page
For instance,	before	description of	the narrator	says	text taken	number when
To illustrate,	because	what is	the writer	reveals	directly out of	the quoted text
In addition,	while	happening	Character	explains	the text and	can be found
Also,	during	when the	name	observes	placed in	written inside
Secondly,	after	quote appears	Author's last	believes	quotation	of parenthesis
Furthermore,	even though	in the text	name	states	marks	without p., pp.,
Likewise,	since		he	argues		pg., or page
Finally,	as		she	asserts		
Moreover,	in the beginning, middle, or end		they	illustrates defends		

Fiction Examples

For example, as the novel's theme unfolds, Atticus helps Scout learn about courage when he tells her, "I wanted you to see what real courage is…It's when you know you're licked before you begin, but you begin anyway" (Lee 116).

Using this Word Bank as an instructional tool is also helpful because it helps me provide my students with quick and specific feedback on how they can improve their evidence sentences. For example, I've noticed that on the first try, students usually do pretty well in including all of the elements from the Word Bank: general transition, set up the situation, describe the situation, indicator, verb, quote, and citation. However, the two elements they collectively most frequently leave out are the indicator and the verb for this model. In providing students with quick feedback, I can read over what they've written so far in the classroom on our writing days and verbally tell them something like this: "That is a great start to your evidence sentence, but it looks like you are missing the indicator and the verb."

In most cases, after I provide students with that feedback, they can look at and analyze their sentence, then revise it so it sounds much better. Once my students revise this part of their sentence and I check it, I encourage them to go back and read their revision aloud to hear the difference it made. Especially when it comes to evidence sentences, students need to hear how the evidence they chose fits within their own writing. The goal is to make it fit seamlessly.

CHAPTER 2

Planning Backward

As a child, I loved playing school. Looking back, I really loved school, and during the summer months, I missed learning. I missed my teachers and classmates, so I tried my best to re-create the school experience at home. I would play the part of teacher, and my younger brother, who is six years younger, would play the role of my student. We'd play school for days and days during the long summer months. I remember using the family's VHS player to record segments on PBS about animals or nature, and then I would create a fill-in-the-blank worksheet for my brother to complete as he watched the video. I would create writing prompts and math problems for him to complete. I was big sister, curriculum designer, teacher, and playmate all in one. However, I have to admit that my brother didn't always want to play. I definitely, in my opinion, had the better role in our game of school.

While I loved playing school, I didn't know anything about effective curriculum planning, engaging teaching strategies, or incorporating research-based pedagogy. But somewhere, deep down, I knew I loved teaching. Now, as a high school English teacher, I combine my love and passion for writing, reading, communicating, and learning with effective curriculum planning to help my students the best way

I can. While I no longer record PBS clips on the family VHS player or hand-draw worksheets, assessments, and paragraph outlines, I still eagerly and excitedly plan and prepare my lessons for my current students. This is where planning backward comes into play.

Starting from the End Goal

One of the key benefits planning backward offers is that it provides teachers with a definitive endpoint—the culminating activity or assessment for the unit. Without planning backward, teachers are more likely to plan lessons and activities that might not build upon one another. Without backward planning, teachers might not prepare students to be entirely successful on the culminating assessment or essay. With writing instruction, planning backward is even more important because writing is a skills-based task that requires thoughtful consideration, scaffolding, and planning. As a type A teacher, whenever I start a unit without direction, without planning backward, I always feel a little lost, and the students likely feel that way as well.

One of the best things a teacher can do when planning a unit or lesson is to plan backward. Planning backward is the act of beginning to plan a unit with the end result in mind. With planning backward, knowing the desired end result is critical. While it is always exciting to start thinking about engaging hook activities and enticing essential questions to capture students' attention and begin your unit, starting with your ultimate end goal is the most effective way to begin planning your instruction.

Before you begin planning your writing unit, start by asking yourself several key questions:

- What do you want your students to learn and produce from this lesson or unit?
- What is the ultimate goal of this lesson or unit?

- What skill do you want students to master by the end of this lesson or unit?

With your answers in mind, you are ready to begin planning backward.

There are three key stages to planning backward, which is sometimes referred to as backward design:

1. Identify the desired results.
2. Determine acceptable evidence.
3. Plan learning experiences and instruction.

Educational research affirms the many benefits of planning backward. With this approach to curriculum design, a teacher starts by addressing standards-based mastery goals and thinking about specific learning objectives. Once they establish a desired learning outcome, the instructor begins to think about the types of work and evidence that form an acceptable demonstration of mastery. Once those two pieces are in place, the teacher can begin planning lessons and activities to help their students meet and achieve the desired unit outcome (Wiggins and McTighe 2005, 346).

To illustrate the benefit of planning backward, let's take a look at grammar. If we want to teach our students about the four sentence types (simple, compound, complex, and compound-complex), quite a bit of alignment and scaffolding is required. First, we would start with the final assessment. In order for our students to be able to demonstrate true mastery of the four sentence types, we ultimately would want them to be able to demonstrate that they can independently write each sentence type. However, before they can write each sentence type independently, we might first have them identify and label sentences on a worksheet. Before students can even do that, we have to go all the way back to the basics: subject and verb. So, having the foresight of the planned summative assessment, we might start our instruction (even at the middle school and high school levels) with a quick review of subjects and verbs, with practice exercises built into the review. From there, we could progress into complete subjects and predicates, and then add phrases and clauses. Along the way, we would also need to teach students about proper comma usage and coordinating conjunctions. So, while the initial concept of a summative assessment about the four sentence types seemed relatively straightforward, planning backward helps us see and carefully plan our units to ensure student success.

Not only does planning backward save time, but it also helps create more cohesive units with lessons that build upon one another to best help students learn and practice the skills and work toward demonstrating mastery. Wiggins and McTighe also assert that implementing a backward design approach to lesson planning helps teachers avoid including ineffective lessons that don't help students learn the skills necessary to achieve desired unit goals.

Whenever I plan to assign a writing assignment—especially formal essays, but even smaller and more informal writing assignments—I find that my students always do better when I take the time and plan backward, carefully crafting each activity to scaffold and set up the next. I cannot even tell you how many times I say things like, "Yes, you can absolutely use what you worked on in class yesterday because that was designed to help you succeed today," or "This is why we completed that exercise in class last week; get those notes and mentor sentences out and use them!" Planning backward effortlessly builds structure and scaffolding through sequence.

While, as mentioned above, Wiggins and McTighe identify three stages for backward design, with planning backward I expand on those areas to create a more robust lesson planning map. Toward that end, the five steps for planning backward are:

1. Identify and establish your main assessment.
2. List out all of the skills that students will need to be successful on the assessment.

3. Arrange the skills in order of complexity, starting with the easiest and ending with the most challenging. This will give you a unit framework.
4. Plan key lessons to bridge the gaps between what the students already know and can do and what they need to do to be successful on the current writing assignment. (As you progress through the school year, you will know your students and their abilities more, so this becomes an easier step throughout the school year.)
5. Have fun filling in the blanks with enjoyable lessons and activities to help your students meet their ultimate goal. Just as teaching writing is challenging and hard work, learning how to write is challenging and hard work for students. It is okay, and even beneficial, if you add some fun, engaging, and collaborative activities to help reinforce certain skills.

Let's dive into each of these steps in more detail.

1. Identify and establish your main assessment.

Remember, with planning backward, the first place to start is with an end goal in mind. That end goal will encompass all the skills and content you want your students to master throughout the entire unit, but especially by the unit's summative assessment. So, as you approach curriculum design, it's crucial to think about your summative assignment, essay prompt, or project, and plan backward from there.

The following are some critical questions you'll want to answer first about your summative assignment before planning your unit:

- What standards will you assess?
- What key skills will you assess?
- How will your summative assignment measure student success in these regards?
- What is your goal for the assignment?

- What criteria will students need to meet to show mastery in the summative assignment?

Knowing the answers to these questions will help you craft and formulate a meaningful and effective writing assignment.

Once you know the standards and skills you want to measure, it's time to craft your final writing assignment. As you craft your final assignment, it is essential to remember that it doesn't always have to be a formal, multiparagraph essay.

There are various ways to assess student writing without having them complete a formal essay.

However, while you want to begin with a summative assignment in mind, every writing assessment and lesson leading up to that cumulative task will also need a series of learning objectives. While learning objectives may be the bane of many teachers' existence, I find that they also help me hone in on the skills I plan on teaching my students. And trust me, when I'm in a time crunch in my own classroom, I also cringe when I realize that I need to add learning objectives to my board. However, research shows that students who have clear and measurable learning objectives for their lessons perform better. Don't worry, though. As I mentioned in the introduction, I've taken the tedious work of wordsmithing your own learning objectives out of the equation for you by providing Daily Learning Objectives for every activity and strategy.

Action Step: Establish the unit goal and craft your writing assignment.

1: Brainstorm to establish the unit goal.

Brainstorming Questions	Your Initial Thoughts
What standards will you assess? What key skills will you assess? How will your summative assignment measure student success in these regards? What is your goal for the assignment? What criteria will students need to meet to show mastery in the summative assignment?	

Once you have established a list of brainstorming questions, begin planning backward to identify all of the crucial skills students will need to learn to succeed. During this step in the process, it is imperative to keep all of your learners in mind and plan backward all the way to the most simplistic skill students will need. From then, you will build on that skill, increasing your lesson complexity, until you get to the final skills required for the summative assessment or ultimate writing assignment.

2: Craft your writing assignment.

Identify and establish your main assessment. How does this assessment speak to the standards you are assessing?	
List out all of the skills students will need to be successful on the assessment. How do those skills relate to the final assessment?	

Arrange the skills in order of complexity. Order these skills, beginning with the easiest and ending with the most challenging. This step provides you with a unit framework.	
Plan key lessons to bridge the gaps. What kinds of lessons and activities will you need to deliver to the students for them to be successful?	
Have fun filling in the blanks. Now that you have a large section of the unit framework created, add fun and exciting activities to keep students engaged and challenged as they work toward mastery.	
What is the writing assignment? Write a specific and measurable writing assignment. How does it speak to the assessment goals?	

Once you develop your final writing assignment and work through the backward planning steps, you may modify your assignment to suit your instruction better. Not only is that perfectly okay, but it is also almost bound to happen. Good teachers get to know their students and their abilities and tailor their instruction and lessons to the students.

2. List all of the key skills students will need to be successful on the assessment.

One of the most crucial planning steps teachers can take here is to be focused and specific when it comes to the skills they expect students to possess. Trust me, I would love for my sophomores to be able to compose a well-written and organized argument essay with a solid thesis statement, perfectly embedded evidence, meaningful commentary, logical academic transitions, and a conclusion paragraph that forces their audience to ponder the topic and life itself. However, I also have to be realistic. Going into my unit, I know that those are skills I will need to teach my students when we are in our argument writing unit.

This is why one of the best approaches for identifying key skills is to keep things simple by focusing only on a few skills at a time. The very art of writing is so complex, it can be daunting. Rather than looking at the whole picture when it comes to writing as an overall practice, I've found much more success by focusing on just a few key skills with every unit and building on those skills throughout the school year. As we discussed in the introduction, think of this strategy as long-term structure, full-year scaffolding.

Let's take a look at a hypothetical argument essay: which character from *Lord of the Flies* is most responsible for the island's ultimate demise?

If I am brainstorming a list of skills that my students will need to know for their very first argument essay in my class, my list of skills might look something like this:

KEY SKILLS: Argument Writing

- Identify and write a claim.
- Support the claim with evidence.
- Identify multiple viewpoints on the issue.
- Embed quotes in writing.

Yes, this is a rather short list, but if this is the first writing assignment students see, it is essential not to overwhelm them. Therefore, I don't recommend starting the year with a multiparagraph essay or even a complete paragraph in many classes. There will always be the exception for seniors, maybe juniors, and honors-level students. At the beginning of the year, though, I have found success with breaking down a writing response into just three sentences and having my students write those three-sentence responses for a few weeks.

> **To read more about how I scaffold my writing responses down to just three sentences at the beginning of the year, see chapter 5.**

Going back to the skills I identified as key for the argumentative writing assignment, I first might want to start with helping students learn to identify claims. Here is a look at how my planning backward internal thought process might work:

> Okay, so students need to be able to write a claim. To do that, they'll need to know what a claim is. To know what a claim is, they will need to know it is a statement that can be argued, is slightly opinionated, and can be supported with reasoning and evidence. From there, my students will need to know what evidence is, but even in knowing what evidence is, they will need to know what reliable and credible evidence is, so I'll need a mini-lesson on that. And then, once they understand what reliable and credible evidence is, students will have to know that the evidence needs to match and support their claim directly and not just be some random quote they pulled from the first article that populated when they did their first Google search. And then, once they've identified evidence that is directly related to and supports their claim, they'll need to know just how much of the source to quote because students definitely like to include those half-page quotes in their essays . . . .

As you can see, this skill identification process quickly expands to many more micro-skills that students will need to learn to approach the main skills you'll be assessing. This branching of skills is a prime example of why planning backward is so crucial for planning, designing, and assessing writing in the secondary ELA classroom. And even more so, it shows why it is important to scaffold skills throughout the year rather than in one essay assignment.

Action Step: Identify your key skills.

	What is the skill?	What else will students need to know to master this skill?
1.		
2.		
3.		
4.		

For this Action Step, it is best to limit your skills to at most four per assignment unless you are building off of previous writing instruction.

---

3. Arrange the skills in order of complexity, starting with the easiest and ending with the most challenging.

By ordering the skills based on their complexity, you set the groundwork for scaffolding and sequencing your instruction for the entire unit. For example, students can't write an argumentative thesis statement without first knowing what a claim is.

You may notice that when you complete the previous step for planning backward, your skills are already in easy-to-difficult order. However, it will sometimes make sense to change the order of some of the skills.

For example, here were the skills I first identified:

KEY SKILLS: Argumentative Writing

- Identify and write a claim.
- Support the claim with evidence.
- Identify multiple viewpoints on the issue.
- Embed quotes in writing.

It makes sense to me to slightly change the order of these skills. To begin, I would say that identifying multiple viewpoints about a topic should be the first and easiest task for this assignment. Before students can even make a claim, they need to know some of the ideas and viewpoints surrounding the issue at hand. Identifying viewpoints is also a task that could be completed collaboratively in class before students write. You'll read more about this process in the next chapter about brainstorming.

Once students can identify multiple viewpoints about a topic, then it would make sense for them to establish their claim. In staying true to argument writing form, students are first supposed to read about the topic and multiple perspectives and then establish their claim. With argument writing, students should never go in with their minds completely made up because it eliminates some of the most important aspects of argument writing, which include researching a topic and synthesizing information with an open mind.

Once students establish their claims, they need to learn how to support those claims with evidence and then embed their evidence in writing. Not only do those skills build off of one another, but they also follow the natural order of writing an essay.

Here is a look at how I would resequence these skills.

KEY SKILLS: Argument Writing

- Identity multiple viewpoints on the issue.
- Identify and write a claim.
- Support the claim with evidence.
- Embed quotes in writing.

> **Action Step: Order your skills based on complexity.**
>
> | | What is the skill? | Rationale for sequencing |
> |----|--------------------|--------------------------|
> | 1. | | |
> | 2. | | |
> | 3. | | |
> | 4. | | |
>
> Now that you have the order of your skills, it is time to plan skill-based lessons to teach your students the essential skills they will need to know to complete the writing task successfully.

4. Plan key lessons to bridge the gaps.

One of the best ways to deliver skill-heavy lessons is through the gradual release of responsibility method of direct instruction. The gradual release of responsibility method is also known as the "I do, we do, you do" method. This approach is tried and true, and it works. The term "gradual release of responsibility" originated more than four decades ago, and it is used to describe a schematic instructional process where the transfer of information happens gradually from teacher to student (Pearson and Gallagher 1983, 317–344). By combining direct instructional strategies with the I do, we do, you do method, students learn key skills, see them applied, work on them as a group, and then practice them independently. This process of aligning focused instruction, guided instruction, and collaborative learning leads to continued learning through the process of independent work (Fisher and Frey 2013).

I've found great success using the gradual release of responsibility method for writing instruction. Implementing this strategy in the classroom helps break down the overwhelming idea of writing an entire composition and makes learning new writing skills more accessible and manageable for students. Let's look at the argument writing skills I've previously identified as crucial for my unit and decide which skill-based lessons I'll need to teach to help my students succeed.

Let's return to the skills we identified and ordered in the previous planning backward step:

KEY SKILLS: Argumentative Writing

- Identity multiple viewpoints on the issue.
- Identify and write a claim.
- Support the claim with evidence.
- Embed quotes in writing.

To teach students that topics, especially those that students use for argument writing, can have multiple perspectives and viewpoints, I first have to identify and explain what a perspective is. Viewpoints and perspectives are the differing opinions and stances people have toward topics. However, after that, students will learn best by using applicable examples of viewpoints they can relate to. I might start with a student-friendly topic that will get them talking. Some of my favorite engaging topics for this include asking students questions like the following:

- Who is the best villain from an animated movie?
- Who is the most powerful superhero?
- What is the best pizza topping?
- Does pineapple belong on a pizza?
- Who makes the best fast-food cheeseburger?
- What kind of sneakers do you like: high top or low top?
- What is the best summertime BBQ: hamburgers or hotdogs?

These topics are fun, engaging, and accessible for students. When I plan key, skill-based lessons around topics—such as supporting ideas and claims with evidence—I always start out with fun topics as my model because they get students interested. Starting with low-stakes viewpoints and perspectives is a quick and easy way to ensure that all students are on the same page, compared to using literature read previously. Furthermore, by focusing on relatable debates, all of our students' energy and brainpower will be focused on developing skills rather than trying to recall a story from several years ago. By showing mastery of the skill using a low-stakes example that is accessible, students build their writing confidence, which transfers over when they begin writing their actual assignment.

For this example, once students know about the viewpoint and claim, it is time to include a lesson with sentence frames showing students how to embed evidence in their writing. It is also essential to check for understanding to ensure that students know that a claim is their opinion on the matter along with a supporting reason. For this, I start with direct instruction, show an example, follow the gradual release method, work with the students on examples from our low-stakes example, and then have my class move on to practicing those skills in their own writing.

Action Step: Plan your skill-based lessons.

	What is the skill?	How will you teach this skill using the gradual release method or a low-stakes, easy-access example?
1.		
2.		
3.		
4.		

After creating skill-based lessons for each key skill, the heavy lifting of backward planning is done, and it is time to fill in the extras with fun and engaging activities!

5. Have fun filling in the blanks.

Once all of your planning is set, because you have your final writing task and know your key, content-rich, and skill-based lessons, it is time to fill in the missing pieces with fun, engaging, and collaborative activities that help students become more confident writers so they get additional practice with the skills.

Whether you are using the low-stakes examples mentioned above, or any other fun and engaging strategies found in this book, running fill-in-the-blanks activities between skill-based lessons really helps students to solidify their understanding through practice, collaboration, and reflection. Far from filler, these activities offer students practice with skills to gain confidence in their writing.

Action Step: Read through the strategies section of this book and note your favorites.

	What is the strategy you wish to implement?	How could you incorporate this in your instruction to teach or reinforce targeted skills?
1.		
2.		
3.		
4.		

That was a quick rundown of backward planning and how I use it to create my writing assessment and then plan effective and engaging lessons to help students become stronger writers.

Planning Backward in My Classroom

Ever since I intentionally set out to implement planning backward in my classroom, I've seen a tremendous difference in my teaching and my students' learning. I've found that I am designing lessons with purpose, and since I share my summative assessment (or at least the gist of it) with my students at the very onset of the unit, they also benefit.

When I first started planning backward, I implemented it within my first unit of the school year with my high school sophomores: literary analysis within short stories. Prior to planning backward, my students and I would go about our merry way, reading different short stories, answering comprehension questions, and pointing out various literary elements. However, at the end of the unit, when it came time to write an essay about the short stories we had read, I realized that my students were not ready to complete the essay because I hadn't intentionally taught them the skills they would need to succeed.

That is when I revamped my short story unit. I started with the assessment I wanted my students to complete: a literary analysis essay examining the author's use of a single literary element and how it helped the author develop the story's theme. Once I had the final essay hammered out, everything about my short story unit became clearer. Not only did I need to teach my students about various literary elements, but I also needed to teach them how to properly embed a quote from the story in their writing. Not only did I need to teach my students about theme versus topic or motif, but I also needed to teach my students how to identify the theme at the beginning, middle, and end of the story. Once I set out and revamped my first unit of the school year, I saw a world of difference in my students' comprehension of the stories, ability to analyze the stories, and in their writing. Everyone won.

CHAPTER 3

Brainstorming

For students, especially students who are struggling, or students with low writing confidence, starting to actually write the essay is often the biggest and most challenging step, especially if students begin the process of writing without even knowing what to write about.

Dedicating instructional time for students to brainstorm is a great way to support all students, especially struggling writers. Plus, it helps model the complete writing process to our students. When students don't take the time to brainstorm their writing beforehand, many problems arise: students stray off topic, students don't respond to the prompt, and students have trouble organizing their ideas.

I've seen it so many times. Students who don't take the time to brainstorm their writing start strong, and throughout their responses, they lose focus. While these students might have answered the prompt initially, the rest of their writing or essay veers off track, and their initial response or claim gets lost. Other times, students who don't brainstorm will completely miss the prompt entirely and write a response that doesn't even address the question initially asked in the prompt in the first place. In other cases, students who don't brainstorm their writing before setting pen to paper (or fingertips to keyboard) will have a response to the prompt embedded somewhere in their writing, but their writing lacks logical organization and is difficult to follow.

However, all of those problems can be avoided with one simple process: brainstorming. In fact, one of the best ways to help students prepare for essay writing at the middle school, high school, and even collegiate levels is by planning deliberate and engaging brainstorming activities during instructional time. In my classroom, brainstorming can be as simple as a quick class warm-up exercise that helps prepare students for the day's work all the way to an elaborate activity where students get together and collaborate as they compile lists of ideas, examples, and potential evidence for an essay.

Regardless of how structured a brainstorming activity is, providing students with an opportunity to brainstorm ideas and evidence for their essays is essential to helping build them into stronger writers because then students will be empowered with the tools they need to succeed. Once they've brainstormed, students will likely stay on topic and answer the prompt because they will have a clear plan for beginning and tackling the assignment. Furthermore, students will have a clear idea of what to write about, and fewer students will be stuck sitting in their seats, not knowing where to start.

When I think about how vital brainstorming before writing is, I think back to my failed CSET examination. The CSET is a test that is part of the California Educator Credentialing Examinations. There is a multiple-subject CSET examination for elementary teacher candidates and subject-specific CSET examinations for single-subject credential holders like me. Since I had not majored in English for my undergraduate degree, I needed to take and pass all four subtests of the English subtest:

- Subtest I: Reading Literature and Informational Texts; Composition and Rhetoric
- Subtest II: Language, Linguistics, and Literacy

- Subtest III: Composition and Rhetoric; Reading Literature and Informational Texts
- Subtest IV: Communications: Speech, Media, and Creative Performances

Altogether, this was one of the hardest tests I've ever taken in my life. However, I figured Subtest IV—Communications: Speech, Media, and Creative Performances—would be a piece of cake with my journalism degree, extensive history with writing, and my experience in student journalism. Much to my delight, my writing prompt was even about journalism. I mean, the stars had completely aligned. The prompt could have been about drama, which I had little experience in. You can imagine my shock when I received my scores. I passed the first two subtests I took, but I failed Subtest IV! I failed the test on the topic on which I earned my degree. I failed the part of the exam in which I was the most confident!

To say I was baffled was an understatement. However, I then deeply reflected on the topic and my response, and I realized where I went astray. I didn't even answer the prompt! I let something so small, and yet so significant, be my downfall. When I opened up the test booklet and read the prompt for Subtest IV, I got so excited to write about journalism that I blabbed on and on about what I knew and loved about journalism and media without even taking a second to sketch out an answer to the prompt! I didn't brainstorm answers to the prompt beforehand; I just started writing. This is something that, as educators, we see so often in the classroom. It is something we repeatedly advise our students not to do! Failing that portion of the CSET was an expensive and time-consuming mistake, but it showed me just how important brainstorming is.

Too often I see students make the same mistakes I did. They see a prompt and immediately begin writing without thinking about an answer to the prompt or staying on topic, and the results show. Some educators think that brainstorming with students means doing the work for them so they don't think critically about prompts, but just like everything else in education, brainstorming is a necessary step we need to teach in the writing process. Brainstorming is one of the most vital parts of the writing process.

The goal of dedicating an entire class period (or even more) to essay brainstorming is to prepare students for the act of writing the essay itself. Going into day one of writing, students should already have a solid idea of their essay topics, their main ideas, and the evidence they will use to support their theses. Brainstorming days should excite the students about writing the essay, which can be helpful if they feel nervous or intimidated to start writing.

I've seen firsthand the difference successful brainstorming can make. One of my all-time favorite class periods I've taught was when I was in my third year of teaching, and I was starting to incorporate more collaborative activities into my repertoire. After some of my students seemed to struggle with a previous essay (their writing was unfocused and repetitive), I realized I needed to dedicate more time to brainstorming. However, I didn't want my students to go at it alone. After all, that led to the downfall of their first essay. So, in the second semester after my freshmen read *The Tragedy of Romeo and Juliet*, I began prepping them for their argument essay. They were tasked with writing an argument paper about who or what ultimately led to the demise of Romeo and Juliet.

To help make brainstorming more fun, I divided my students into small groups of three to four students and assigned each group a different character or contributing factor. Then, I gave each group a piece of poster paper and tasked my students with writing down as many reasons and quotes as possible that supported the idea that their assigned person or topic led to the protagonists' demise. I walked around the room as students worked. At first, the class was pretty quiet because students were rereading parts of the text, but then the magic started to happen. After about fifteen minutes, students were talking with one another about their topic and their supporting evidence. They read passages from the text aloud to each other and discussed whether that piece of evidence fit their case. Soon after, they began using the markers, and more than one student contributed to the posters at a time. I had the students wrap up ten minutes before the bell rang. Each student group shared their topic, one reason, and one supporting quote aloud. After the students left for the day, I hung up the posters on the walls so my students could refer back to them the following class period.

Part of building strong writers is centered on preparing and empowering them. By spending one entire instructional day with my students in a collaborative setting, working toward brainstorming ideas for their essays, I got them excited about their writing. My students entered class the following day with ideas swirling about their heads. They felt prepared, and they were empowered to write.

Scaffolding the Brainstorming Process

DAILY LEARNING OBJECTIVE: Using the provided text or passages, students will work together to identify, record, and organize potential ideas and evidence for their essays.

Scaffolding instruction is a crucial step in lesson design so students are introduced to new, complex ideas one step at a time. Similar to how a distance runner cannot just go out and run a marathon without proper training, students can't just digest complex instruction without the training, the crucial steps needed to be successful. I like to scaffold brainstorming strategies in my classroom to build student confidence. Accordingly, toward the beginning of the year, the brainstorming strategies and activities I include in my classroom are more structured and provide students with more guidance than brainstorming activities later in the year.

1. Give students a list of ideas.

At the beginning of the year, or for the first formal writing assignment of the school year, I might scaffold brainstorming by providing my student groups with a comprehensive list of ideas they might write about. I then offer students a chance to discuss and evaluate these potential essay ideas in groups.

For example, I recently worked on a gothic literature unit with my students. Leading up to that essay, we had already read, analyzed, and discussed four or five short stories or poems that fit within this genre, and students needed to synthesize the information they'd read and write about common gothic literature elements. The essay prompt was for them to write an informative essay about which elements are commonly found in gothic literature. Accordingly, I provided them with this list of gothic elements:

1. Intensely emotional
2. Damsel in distress
3. A suspenseful or eerie mood
4. Isolated setting
5. Supernatural and paranormal activity
6. Ominous weather
7. Burdened male protagonist
8. Ancient prophecy
9. Women threatened by a tyrannical or powerful male
10. Macabre

While this list of ten was rather exhaustive, I did not expect students to write an essay that included all ten elements. That's too much, especially at the beginning of the school year. Instead, to help students brainstorm for a standard five-paragraph essay, I directed them to first rank the list (either in order of importance, or better yet, based on their understanding and comfort with each topic) and discuss those ranks in groups. This activity took no more than five to ten minutes, and it initiated a discussion about the essay.

From there, I asked student groups to select the top three elements and add as many ideas as they could to support their chosen three. For example, if students chose ominous weather, damsel in distress, and isolated setting, they would add details to each topic. For ominous weather, students might add phrases like "dark and stormy night" and "ominous rumbling in the distance."

To take this brainstorming activity to the next level, once scaffolding had been put in place, I might ask student groups to find specific examples of each of these elements from stories we just read in class.

Action Step: Identify your prompt and generate possible topics.

What is your writing prompt?	
What ten ideas could students write about?	1. 2. 3. 4. 5. 6. 7. 8. 9. 10.

Remember, of the ten possible topics, students will rank them and choose no more than three to write about.

2. Give students a list of quotes.

Once students complete the above activity, they can move to a slightly more advanced group brainstorming activity: selecting quotes to support their essays' main ideas. Just as I provide my students with a list of potential topics at the start of the essay-writing process, I also provide them with an exhaustive list of potential quotes they could use in their essays. This is helpful for the students because even though they have a list of quotes, they still choose which quotes they want to use. They are still selecting the quotes that best support their essays' arguments. Providing students with a list of potential quotes is a great scaffold to help students see firsthand the power of choosing compelling and meaningful evidence in their writing!

I must emphasize here that providing a list of quotes absolutely does not mean doing the work for my students. My students are still the ones who will be doing all the heavy lifting in the essay-writing process. By the *end* of the school year, the ultimate goal is to provide students with enough scaffolding, tools, and instruction to find supporting evidence independently. In the first couple months of the school year, however, these scaffolds and strategies lay the foundation so we can build our students into strong writers.

So, building off the same writing prompt about key elements found in gothic literature, I provided my students with a list of quotes from short stories we previously read: "The Tell-Tale Heart" by Edgar Allan Poe, "The Monkey's Paw" by W. W. Jacobs, and "The Feather Pillow" by Horacio Quiroga. For the most recent iteration of this assignment, I decided to provide my students with four quotes from each story. That list included more quotes than students might use because I wanted to spark discussion among my student groups about which quotes they should use, why a quote would be the best one to support their topic, and how they might explain the quote's connection to the essay prompt.

From this list of quotes, I directed students to select just one or two from each story and write them down on paper. I then asked my students to talk with one another about why they chose one quote over the other and to jot down a short list that connects the quote to the essay prompt.

Again, providing quotes did not involve doing the heavy lifting for my students. While I did provide my students with the actual quotes for their writing, they were the ones who selected the best quotes. They were the ones who made critical connections between quotes and essay topics. They were the ones who ultimately provided all of the analysis of their quotes. By giving students a list of quotes, I helped them learn the process of how to perform all these critical skills. They started with a building block and worked from there.

As the year goes on, your students will no longer need such building blocks. In fact, you might even have some students in the early days who want to bring in additional quotes they remember from the reading. Sometimes I offer a challenge to my students at this phase of brainstorming by telling them they can follow that impulse. Offering these small class challenges is a great way to see which students want to expand their writing skills and who might be interested in pursuing an honors or AP class. Challenges are also less intimidating because they are optional. Even if students just think about a challenge, they are starting to open up their minds to growing as a writer.

Teacher Tip: Offering small, optional challenges like this is a great way to add differentiation to your classroom.

> **Action Step: Identify your writing prompt and list of stories you read (keep it short at first) and come up with four quotes from each for your students.**
>
> | | |
> |---|---|
> | What is your writing prompt? | |
> | What three stories did you read? | 1.
2.
3. |
> | What are four quotes you can use from the first story? | 1.
2.
3.
4. |
> | What are four quotes you can use from the second story? | 1.
2.
3.
4. |
> | What are four quotes you can use from the third story? | 1.
2.
3.
4. |
>
> A helpful tip for providing students with four different quotes is to keep each quote relatively simple at first. You'll want to keep each example quote to no more than a few sentences each. After some practice, students will be ready to select quotes from longer, preselected passages.

3. Give students a passage.

The third scaffolding step for the brainstorming process is to gradually release the responsibility of finding topics and quotes to your students while still providing them with support. To do this, I like to provide students with carefully selected passages from the text that include many topics related to the essay prompt. It is important to remember that this is still part of scaffolding the brainstorming process for students, but it leaves students responsible for finding topics and then eventually selecting quotes. Providing a passage allows students to focus on relevant information and eliminates extraneous material that can be distracting, confusing, or overwhelming. Additionally, when students move on to peer editing, these passages provide the basis for models and comparisons.

This next step of scaffolding the brainstorming process empowers students to build on the skills they've been developing in your class without completely setting them off on their own.

For example, another of my classes worked on a genre-based analysis essay for which I wanted my students to identify common elements or archetypes found in dystopian literature. For this essay, we'd already read and discussed "There Will Come Soft Rains" and "The Veldt" by Ray Bradbury and "The Lottery" by Shirley Jackson.

In building on this next step in brainstorm scaffolding, I provided my students with three lengthier passages they could read in small groups. All of these passages also contained multiple examples of dystopian genre elements. Depending on how much time you have in your own classes, you might give student groups one, two, or all three passages. Students in these groups should then work together to identify and list dystopian elements. To elevate this brainstorming activity, have each student group share the passage they read, one dystopian element they found, and explain why they chose it.

> **Action Step: Identify your writing prompt, the stories you read together as a class, and the reading passages from each story you want your students to read.**
>
> | | |
> |---|---|
> | What is your writing prompt? | |
> | What three stories did you read? | 1.
 2.
 3. |
> | What passage will you have students read from story 1? | |
> | What passage will you have students read from story 2? | |
> | What passage will you have students read from story 3? | |
>
> A helpful tip is to look for passages that contain multiple examples of the elements you want students to find. Some helpful passages for a literature-based writing prompt introduce the setting, provide examples of characterization, or illustrate the story's central conflict.

Teacher Tip: When facilitating group brainstorming activities in the classroom, it is helpful to shake things up and vary how students write, record, and present information. So you can also ask students to find and explain quotes from the passages that help answer the prompt and then record their answers on a collaborative digital presentation, a piece of butcher paper, a whiteboard, mini-whiteboards, sticky notes, Google Slides, or even large sheets of paper. This helps boost student engagement and prevent students from tuning out because they are doing the same thing activity after activity.

Advanced Brainstorming Activities

DAILY LEARNING OBJECTIVE: Students will work (either collaboratively or individually) to learn how to find and brainstorm information, organize it logically, and be able to use it for a future writing assignment.

When I plan brainstorming activities in my classroom, I use two types: group and individual. I begin the year with group brainstorming (and even whole-class brainstorming) to model the brainstorming process to my students and to get them actively discussing the text or the prompt in class. As we progress throughout the year, I include more individual brainstorming activities to assess each student separately. I often like to include both types of brainstorming activities in my classroom before we start drafting. If students are working on the first essay of a new school year, I especially want to incorporate collaborative essay brainstorming. This is because, even though my students might have brainstormed in the past, it is a new activity in my classroom with this particular group of students. Working on collaborative brainstorming at the beginning of the school year allows me to walk around and monitor student progress. I can also see which students are leading the group and who might need more assistance with the process.

Once my students have more practice with brainstorming, I incorporate additional strategies to promote individual efficacy within all of my students. For example, after several group brainstorming activities, I might try the think, pair, share strategy so each student has some time to develop the skill individually.

Common group brainstorming supplies

Using a variety of classroom supplies and switching things up with each new group brainstorming activity helps me avoid monotony in my classroom and keep students engaged:

- Sticky notes
- A large roll of white butcher paper

- Large paper (think 11- by 17-inch and 17- by 22-inch)
- Markers
- Mini-whiteboards
- Extra whiteboard markers
- Digital collaborative tools (such as Google Slides or Padlet)

Group Brainstorming Activities

Group brainstorming can be done with a partner, in small groups, or in a whole-class setting. I have my classroom set up as six table groups of six students each, which is very helpful for group activities. Typically, I like to create my student groups with a good heterogeneous mix of ability levels and learning styles. To help my students feel more comfortable in their table groups, I take some time to complete team-building activities like the cup-stacking challenge, and I also give them fun attendance questions to discuss so they become more comfortable with one another. This helps prevent students from trying to opt out of collaborative work, especially since they've built a relationship with one another at their tables.

The Poster Project

Approximate time: 40–60 minutes
Supplies needed: Chart paper, butcher paper, or poster paper; markers
Class activity: Group activity turned whole-class activity

1) Remind students about the importance of brainstorming. Stress the importance of brainstorming and tell students that this is where we get out all ideas that might be related to what we are writing about. Emphasize that there are no bad ideas and that we can also go through and select key information later.
2) Divide students into groups of three to five.
3) Supply each group with markers and a large piece of paper (torn-off butcher paper or 17- by 22-inch paper).

4a) Assign each group a different topic for the essay and have the groups create a poster representing that topic. Students may offer words, phrases, key points, supporting quotes, partial explanations, and illustrations for their group's assigned topic.

4b) If you are in a crunch or want to add more accountability to the activity, supply students with scrap paper and glue, and then students write their contributions on the scrap paper and glue it to the poster. Or ask each student to name their contribution on the paper.

5) After student groups complete their posters, have each group present their poster to the class. This can be done informally from the students' seats or more formally at the front of the classroom.

When I run this activity, I've found that it helps to give students a minimum checklist of items to keep adding information to their posters. For example, I might have students write ten keywords, and five phrases, including four cited quotes, and two images. I give my students almost the entire class period to work on their posters. This might seem like too much time, but during the class period, I go around the room, check on each group, and suggest additional points to consider. Since the main goal of this project is to brainstorm information collaboratively for their essays, I like to keep the presentations informal and simple. Students share their posters from their seats.

The posters students create can offer support throughout the writing process. After every group shares, I display the posters throughout the classroom for additional support. When students eventually draft their writing, I encourage them to get up, walk around, and view the posters for additional ideas and support. If I notice a student sitting and not writing for an abnormally long time, I encourage them to go read through some of the posters. That helps reset the student, and it gives them additional time to process the information.

> **Action Step: Identify your writing prompt and the elements you want to include on each poster.**
>
> | | |
> |---|---|
> | What is your writing prompt? | |
> | What elements do you want to be included on the poster? | |
> | How many of these elements do you want to be included on the poster? | |
>
> Here is a list of potential items to include on the student posters:
>
> - Keywords
> - Phrases
> - Quotes from the text
> - Quotes from reliable sources
> - Illustrations
> - Explanations
> - Definitions
> - Paraphrased examples from the text
> - Connections to another story
> - Connections to the real world
> - Quotes about the topic by a philosopher, historian, politician, or author

Sticky Note Stampede

Approximate time: 20–40 minutes
Supplies needed: Sticky notes, markers, a whiteboard, or a place to stick notes
Class activity: Group activity turned whole-class activity

1) Place students in pairs or small groups.
2) Provide each pair or group with several sticky notes.
3) Discuss the upcoming essay prompt with the class.
4) Direct students in the groups to work together to brainstorm main ideas, supporting details, examples, quotes, and

explanations that support the topic. Students should write just one thing per note.

5) Ask each student group to share their ideas aloud.
6) After the groups share their responses, write down the three or four most popular ideas they brainstormed on the whiteboard and direct students to place their sticky notes on the board under the idea that makes the most sense.
7) Give students several minutes to discuss where they will place each note, and then have one group member add their notes to the board to create an organized outline of their ideas on the whiteboard.

Idea 1	Idea 2	Idea 3	Idea 4
Students place their idea, quote, and explanation sticky notes underneath the matching ideas. This helps students see how they can organize their ideas in the essay. Each of the ideas students brainstorm together can turn into a body paragraph or reason that supports their thesis.			

If you introduce this brainstorming strategy at the beginning of the year, students might be reluctant to include quotes and explanations in their notes. You might find more main ideas and supporting details. To mitigate this issue, try providing students with a checklist of items they must include.

I like using the whiteboard for the outline portion of this activity because I can draw large boxes or arrows on it to help students visually organize their ideas. For example, I might link a quote to an explanation and explain to my students why those ideas fit well together.

As with the posters in the previous activity, keep the sticky notes up on display for the entire essay-writing process. This will provide your students with additional information that might benefit their essays.

Teacher Tip: To add more structure to this brainstorming activity, add in color-coding. Assign each group a different topic, and each topic will have its unique-color sticky note. It is okay if multiple groups have the same topic. In fact, that is quite beneficial because it will help add to the ideas brainstormed. Then, when students post sticky notes on the board, they will have the information classified. By adding more structure, you are guaranteeing that a wider variety of topics will be brainstormed.

Action Step: Identify your writing prompt and multiple supporting ideas for the students.

What is your writing prompt?	
What are potential topics that students can write about for this essay prompt?	1. 2. 3. 4.

When brainstorming a list of potential topics, it is always best to include more topics than students can write about. For example, if you assign a four-paragraph essay where each body paragraph constitutes one topic, it would be a good idea to present students with four different topics so they have more choices. Also, that helps break up the monotony of essay grading!

Gallery Walk

Approximate time: 40–60 minutes
Supplies needed: Chart paper or poster paper, markers
Class activity: Group activity turned whole-class activity

1) Place chart paper, butcher paper, or poster board on the walls. You can also designate different portions of your whiteboard for student answers if you have enough colors of dry-erase markers.

2) Designate each piece of chart paper or poster board as a different potential supporting idea.
3) Divide students into small, even-ish groups of about four to six students.
4) Assign a designated color marker for each group.
5) Provide student groups with time to brainstorm each topic at their tables or desks.
6) Direct students to get up and move around the classroom, adding their ideas about each topic to the appropriate paper.
7) Have students rotate around the room at each station/piece of chart paper. When students move to a new designated station, they should first read all of the contributions prior groups have added. Then, using their designated-color markers, students will write their ideas on the paper, being conscious of not repeating the same information already on the paper.
8) Encourage student groups to always add new information to the paper, even if it is a new quote, new insight, or a different way to view the topic. This task will increase in difficulty as they progress through the stations.
9) With about ten minutes left in the class period, ask students to summarize their final poster, either aloud or in writing. Completing this step aloud helps all of the students in the room see different supporting ideas they could potentially write about. Completing it on paper helps individual students organize and reflect on the ideas in front of them.

When I run this activity, to help keep order in the classroom, I have students stay at each station for a predetermined set time, perhaps five minutes, and then rotate all at once in a given direction. This helps maintain order and eliminate confusion. However, if you complete this activity many times throughout the year, you can switch things up and have students manage their time and rotations. For example, you can tell students they must make at least three meaningful contributions to each poster, and there can be no more than two student groups at each poster.

Again, these posters are gifts meant to keep on giving. Keep them up on the walls during the essay-writing process so students can access them at all points of the unit.

> **Action Step: Identify your writing prompt, then determine the topics for each station, how many groups you will have, how you will set up the walk, and which colors each student group will use.**
>
> | | |
> |---|---|
> | What is your writing prompt? | |
> | What will the topics of each poster be? | |
> | How many student groups will you have? | |
> | How will you set up the walk? (Will it be on butcher paper, will you use portions of your whiteboard, etc.?) | |
> | What color will each group have? | |
> | What elements can student groups add to the posters? | |
>
> One way to help traffic flow better during this group brainstorming activity is to have one extra poster or station than the number of student groups. To help eliminate redundant student responses, you can also have two posters for each topic; that way, students see fewer responses when they walk up to the poster.

> **Teacher Tip:** If there are quite a few different options for topics, or if you are in a pinch for time, students do not have to visit every single station. You can instruct your students to complete, for example, four of the six stations and then return to their seats.

> **Teacher Tip:** Another way to implement this activity in the classroom, especially if your room is set up in table groups, is to have each table group work on their table's topic as a "home topic." At the end of the activity, each group will read and evaluate all of the information on their "home topic" paper, circle the top five ideas, and then share those five contributions with the class.

Brainstorming Stations

Approximate time: 40–60 minutes
Supplies needed: Different instructions for each station
Class activity: Group activity turned whole-class activity

1) Set up essay brainstorming sessions throughout the room. Each station should include a different essay topic, task, or passage to read through and draw information from. For example, one station may require students to think of as many examples as possible to support a topic sentence, and another station might require students to read closely to find a supporting quote.
2) Divide your students equally into the number of stations you've created. I typically have groups of three to six students.
3) Give each student a "recording sheet." It doesn't even need to be fancy or formal; a blank piece of lined paper is sufficient.
4) Prompt students to divide this recording sheet into several sections equal to the number of stations.
5) Instruct your students to rotate through the brainstorming stations in small groups, gathering as much information as possible for their essays. To help students transition from one station to the next, I like to give them a one-minute and a

thirty-second reminder. This helps students finish up their current task and move on to the next one without feeling rushed.
6) As students rotate, they will take their recording sheet with them and keep adding to it. By the time they complete all of the stations, they will have a lot of useful information on their recording sheet.
7) At the end of the class, discuss what students learned and brainstorm.

Sample Implementation

Before running this activity, I worked with my class to annotate and rewrite our essay prompt. First, we read the essay prompt in a whole-group setting. Then, students annotated the essay prompt by underlining what the prompt was asking of them and highlighting key action phrases. Next, I had the students work with partners to rewrite the essay prompt in their own words while maintaining its original integrity. This prestation activity helped students understand what is expected of them during the essay.

Once students rewrote the prompt in their own words, I shared potential essay topics with them. This step ensured that students were on the same page and that they began the station activity ready to brainstorm. Because we were writing an essay about who or what is responsible for Romeo and Juliet's deaths, I shared the list of possible culprits.

For activity stations, I made one station for each person or thing that potentially contributed to Romeo and Juliet's deaths. At these stations, students read an excerpt from the text, discussed how each person or element could have contributed to the protagonists' deaths, and found quotes to use as supporting details. Since there were ten different options, students didn't ultimately make it to every station, and that was okay. The beneficial aspect of this activity was that students had exposure to multiple possible answers to the prompt. So, even if they only made it to three stations, they brainstormed for more than what they needed for the essay. This was also where student choice came into play. Students feel more empowered when they have a choice in their work. If students have a choice of stations, they will have more buy-in to the activity.

> **Action Step: Identify your writing prompt, the task for each station, and how students will record their responses.**
>
> | | |
> |---|---|
> | What is your writing prompt? | |
> | How many stations will you have? | |
> | How much time will students have at each station? | |
> | What are the directions/tasks for each station? | 1.
2.
3.
4.
5.
6. |
> | How will students record their work and contributions from each station? | |
>
> A low-prep way to create a station recording sheet is to have students use a piece of their own paper. If there are four stations, have the students fold the piece of paper into quarters and number each box or rectangle. If there are six stations, have the students fold their papers so there are an even number of boxes. If you have an off number of stations, you can still do this. Instruct the students to number the boxes and then label the last one "reflection." You can provide time at the end of the class for students to put together everything they learned and discussed from all of the stations in the reflection box.

Jigsaw Reading

Approximate time: 40–60 minutes
Supplies needed: The assignment reading, a piece of paper for each group
Class activity: Group activity turned whole-class activity

Jigsaw reading is a beneficial brainstorming strategy if you are trying to cover a lot of material at once.

1) Select several sections of text from a key reading.
2) Divide your students into small groups and assign each group a section of text to read.
3) Direct students, as groups, to read the text, discuss it, formulate the most important information that will help them answer the prompt, identify potential quotes they can use for their essays, and explain how those quotes connect to the essay prompt. As each student works in their group, they will want to jot down the information they learned on their own piece of paper. Provide twenty-five to thirty minutes for this step.
4) Have each student group share and present their information.
5) Once students are done exploring and representing a passage, rearrange your student groups so each newly formed group includes one member from each original group. Then, reassign each group to one of the sections of text.
6) Once the new student groups are set, provide time for the students to share and learn from one another. Students sharing information with their new groups will find that the initial notes they took come in handy as they present the information to their peers.

> **Action Step: Identify your writing prompt and select the passages for the jigsaw read.**
>
> | | |
> |---|---|
> | What is your writing prompt? | |
> | How many different sets of passages do you want to include in the activity? | |
> | Which passages will you include for this brainstorming activity? | |
>
> When selecting reading passages, it is helpful to keep them about the same length. It is impossible to have them all be the same exact length, but keeping the lengths similar is helpful for pacing this activity.

Partner Interview

Approximate time: 10–30 minutes
Supplies needed: Printed-out questions for each partner group
Class activity: Partner activity

This is really just an activity to get students thinking and talking about writing, but the process helps them gather ideas. By talking about their own writing and by listening to their partner discuss their writing, students should gain some new insight about their topic and their writing.

1) Partner students up.
2) Direct students to interview one another about their essays.

Here are some sample questions students can ask and respond to during the partner interview activity:

- What is your essay about?
- What side or topic do you feel most strongly about and why?
- Who or what do you think is the best reason? Why? (This one can be more prompt-specific.)
- What kind of evidence do you think you'll need to support your thesis sentence?

- What kind of hook or connection will you use to connect this to the real world?
- What kind of tone are you hoping to convey in your essay? Why?

3) As students participate in the partner interview activity, instruct them to record their partner's answers to the best of their ability.

> **Teacher Tip:** This brainstorming activity would make for a great bell ringer at the start of a class period once you have already introduced an essay prompt. Even if you've already completed another individual or group brainstorming activity in class, this activity will offer new perspectives to students. You could also turn this into a speed dating kind of activity where students go around the room and briefly interview three or four students to get more perspectives.

Individual Brainstorming Activities

While facilitating group brainstorming activities in the classroom as part of teaching the writing process is a beneficial and successful part of teaching students how to write, sometimes, dedicating an entire day to brainstorming just might not be feasible. Plus, students need to be able to brainstorm ideas on their own without the assistance of a group, partner, or teacher. Just like I could not brainstorm collaboratively with my peers before diving into the writing portion of Subtest IV of the CSET, there will be times when students will not have that opportunity, either. While these individual brainstorming activities can be stretched out to take twenty minutes or more, they can also be quick activities during a bell-ringer activity.

Mind Map

Approximate time: 15–30 minutes
Supplies needed: Paper and writing supplies (some students may prefer markers or colorful pens)
Class activity: Individual or partner activity

A mind map is a visual tool that helps students brainstorm, classify, and organize information. It represents their thoughts, ideas, and concepts in a hierarchical and interconnected manner, and it is a very useful tool for visual learners.

1) Give each student a blank piece of paper.
2) In the center, instruct students to write the essay prompt and circle it.
3) To add more structure, ask students to annotate the essay prompt by underlining and highlighting key aspects of the prompt. This will represent the mind map's central idea.
4) From there, instruct students to create branches that radiate outward from the central topic and to fill those branches with ideas, topics, illustrations, and thoughts.
5) From here, students can then create sub-branches and keep expanding their mind map.

An essay-brainstorming mind map might include the following:

- Central topic
- Main ideas
- Supporting details
- Quotes
- Explanations
- Illustrations and doodles
- Words and phrases

KWL Chart

Approximate time: 5–20 minutes or more
Supplies needed: A piece of paper folded vertically into a KWL chart for each student
Class activity: Individual

Part of brainstorming is the act of sitting and thinking—a skill many of our students either lack or struggle with. A know, want, learned (KWL) chart is another tried-and-true, research-based strategy for essay brainstorming, especially for argument and research-based writing.

1) Give each student a blank sheet of paper.
2) Instruct students to fold that paper into three vertical sections and label each section:
   - K: What I KNOW about the subject
   - W: What I WANT to know about the subject
   - L: What I LEARNED about the subject
3) Pace students and give them a dedicated amount of time to consider and complete each section. This helps ensure that students aren't rushing through the process.
4) For the K section, it is important to stress that students shouldn't write what they *think* they know; they must write down what they know. They can do this by using bullet points or even complete sentences. This step allows students to access their prior knowledge on the subject.
5) In the W section, students begin to plan their research. Have students generate questions and explore their curiosity surrounding the subject. This portion of the KWL chart helps students formulate research questions, set expectations around their learning, and focus their research around specific areas of interest or gaps in their prior knowledge.
6) Following the W section, give the students independent work time. Perhaps they need to do some research on databases, or maybe they need to go back and read selected passages from a short story or novel. However, when they set out to do their

work, they are prepped and ready. They know what they know, and they know what they want to know.

7) Students won't complete the L portion of the KWL chart. Once they've had time to research and reread information, students should complete the L section by adding what they've learned throughout their independent research.

> **Teacher Tip:** Help your students classify the information they've included in their KWL chart by color-coding it. Instruct students to use three different-colored markers, colored pencils, or crayons and underline and circle each item with a connected color. For example, if they choose green as their first color, they would circle or underline something in green. Then, they would go through the entire KWL chart and circle or underline every other piece of information related to their first annotation in green. For example, students might highlight the benefits of a topic in green. Within their KWL chart, anything considered a benefit would be highlighted in green. Then, students would move on to a new color and circle or underline something else and repeat the process. For example, students might choose to highlight any information associated with risks in orange, and all of the risks would be highlighted in orange. The key here is for students to classify the information as they go and color-code related ideas, which will make organizing their paper easier when they get to the outlining process.

> **Teacher Tip:** Use the 3-2-1 strategy described below as a bell-ringer activity in your classroom when you spend multiple days researching and reviewing information for an argument or research-based essay.

1) Ask students to write down three things they learned about their topic already. This will help them remember, activate their memory, and recall what they've already learned and looked up.

2) Instruct students to write down two things they want to learn more about. In doing so, students will set goals and expectations for their day's work.
3) Direct students to write one question that they still have about the topic. The question can be a wonder, a curiosity, or a general question.

Writing Lists

Approximate time: 3–5 minutes
Supplies needed: A piece of paper for each student
Class activity: Individual

I like to complete this essay brainstorming activity as a class warm-up or a bell ringer. We all know what a list is: a record or a catalog of items, usually similar to one another in some way, written vertically down a piece of paper. Lists can be numbered or distinguished by bullet points and consist of words or phrases. Having students write quick lists is simple, easy to execute, and requires relatively little preparation work. Writing lists for brainstorming can be an introductory activity for another brainstorming activity.

Writing lists is a helpful brainstorming strategy because it begins to activate the brain so students begin to access their prior knowledge about a topic.

Students will first start out strong. They will write their lists relatively easily, and at first, the ideas should come to them rather quickly, especially if students are considering a topic they already have some prior knowledge about (for argument-based essays, this is one reason why it is a good idea to provide students with a choice of topics). However, as the seconds tick on, students will slow down and run out of steam. This is a good thing! This state of not immediately knowing what to write down next helps students begin to think about the topic in new ways. They will start to wonder about the topic and without even realizing it, they might even begin to formulate research questions in their minds as well. I encourage students to push through and continue to think, even when it gets tough. I also let them know they can write down any questions they have if they need to.

Writing lists is a quick and easy brainstorming activity; walking around the room as students work is also essential. Gauging timing in the classroom can be quite challenging, and you might need to add or subtract time. Just monitor your students; when the majority start to slow down, it might be time to wrap up the activity.

> **Teacher Tip:** Since writing a list does not take long, this activity is great for stacking into another activity. If you use the list-making brainstorming activity as a class starter, you can then have students group together and use their lists to collaborate on another brainstorming activity.

> **Teacher Tip:** If you want a more whole-class approach with students' lists, bring everyone back from their independent work for a class discussion. Ask for student volunteers to slowly read their lists aloud. As they do, write (or have another student write) items on the whiteboard or type them up in a shared document. You don't need to repeat any items. Keep asking for more student volunteers to share items from their lists that are not listed on the board yet. Eventually, you will have compiled a large list the entire class contributed to.

Freewriting

Approximate time: 5–10+ minutes
Supplies needed: A piece of paper for each student
Class activity: Individual

Like writing lists, freewriting is another great essay-brainstorming activity that can take place at the start of the class period as a warm-up. Whenever I engage my students in freewriting, I emphasize that I am not looking for correct grammar or spelling and that their ideas do not need to be organized in any way. I let them know that the purpose of this is a "brain dump." They are to dump out as much information about their topic as possible on their paper.

What sets freewriting apart from list writing is that, where the list focuses on singular and simpler ideas, a freewrite helps students focus on larger issues and begin to make that connection between them right away.

For freewrites, I like to set a timer. To help ease any anxiety that might come along with timers in the classroom, though, I let students know that it is perfectly okay if they don't finish in time. However, I do expect students to be actively writing or thinking about writing (meaning it isn't a time to check out) the entire time. For some students, this is a struggle. I encourage students who run out of ideas to begin writing questions about the subject. They can write questions about its history or questions about how it works, or questions about its future. They can write questions about anything relating to it.

> **Teacher Tip:** Once students are done with their freewrite, you can take this activity to the next level by providing students with time to read what they wrote. After students read their responses, instruct them to go back and highlight or circle one or two things that are either the most interesting or that stand out to them.

Questioning

Approximate time: 5–15 minutes
Supplies needed: A piece of paper for each student
Class activity: Individual

Similar to the list-making brainstorming activity, questioning is another great individual brainstorming activity that is quick and easy. Give students a little time in class to think about their topics and write down any questions they have about them. It is important to remind students that there are no silly questions; even simple and rudimentary questions can help them expand their ideas and thinking later on.

For those classes that are difficult to motivate, where a time-based brainstorming activity might not work, challenge your students to write a predetermined number of questions. To help prep students for writing questions, I suggest writing down the typical question words—who, what, when, why, and how—for students. Encourage them to write down a single question for each type.

CHAPTER 4

Outlines

During every teacher meeting I have with my PLC at school, when we discuss student writing, we always have one key observation: so many of our students either fail to answer the prompt entirely, or they start strong but quickly veer off topic. That happens when students rush to get through their writing and don't take the time needed to outline their thoughts.

Most students don't intrinsically know how to outline an essay. It is something we must teach them. By teaching students to slow down during the writing process and how to outline an essay, we are providing them with an additional tool for success. We are helping students become stronger writers because then they will stay on topic and answer the essay prompt.

As an educator who teaches students how to write, I view the outline as the most vital piece of the writing process. In class, I tell students that as they are working on their outlines, they are putting in all the hard work now. I let them know that once they piece together their outline, all that is left is flushing out the details and tying together the loose strings. Depending on my students, their ability levels, and how much time we spent brainstorming, it is helpful to dedicate at least one whole class day to essay outlining so students do not rush through this crucial process.

However, just like teaching students the process of how to brainstorm, teaching students how to effectively outline an essay also requires scaffolding that takes place throughout the year. At the beginning of the school year, students need more structure and support to begin an essay outline. With consistent work and practice throughout the year using those structures and supports, the goal is to help students eventually complete an essay outline without any of the supports.

Scaffolding the Outlining Process

DAILY LEARNING OBJECTIVE: Working through the writing process, students will learn how to use previously brainstormed information and organize it logically to form an essay outline.

In my classroom, to begin the scaffolding process, my students complete a more detailed, structured outline before they begin their first drafts, especially at the start of the school year. And I mean, this outline is *detailed*! It is almost the entire essay! Pedagogical research also confirms the numerous benefits of students creating a detailed outline before the drafting process. Detailed outlines help students because this helps them lay the groundwork for their essays, and it naturally guides them to organize their academic essays before writing them (Medina 1994, 8–9). And now, in today's era of teaching, this type of essay outline, especially when completed in class and on paper, helps combat plagiarism and the use of AI.

When I teach students to make outlines, I've found that it is best to provide them with more structure and support at the start of this process. Typically, you hear less is more, but not for the first time students outline an essay in your class. With proper scaffolding, students develop specific, structured, and focused outlines for every part of their essays. That is why I like to use a two-column, structured outline with my students. On the left-hand side, I label every part of each paragraph, provide a desired sentence length, and then give students a description of what they need to include. Students then use the right-hand side of the essay outline to either hand write in or type their content.

As you see in the outline below, the structured outline provides students with step-by-step guidance as they organize and outline their thoughts and ideas. Remember, this is a basic essay outline for teaching students how to write academic essays. Typically, students start with a five-paragraph, formulaic essay. Once they can write within those parameters, I have students work on less formulaic essays.

ESSAY INTRODUCTION	
HOOK **One sentence** The hook should be a thought-provoking way to intrigue your reader. Consider starting with an interesting or shocking fact or an anecdote. Avoid starting your essay with a question. If you can only think of questions, turn your question into an interesting statement.	
BACKGROUND INFORMATION **Two to five sentences** The background information for your essay should provide your audience with enough information about your essay's topic so they understand your argument. If you are writing about a story, provide the title, author, genre, and summary of the story. If you are writing about a subject, provide some brief history and key details.	
THESIS STATEMENT **One sentence** The thesis statement should contain all of the information in your essay in a detailed, concise statement. The thesis statement should be arguable and defendable.	

BODY PARAGRAPHS 1-3	
TOPIC SENTENCE **One sentence** *This sentence should clearly state the topic of your paragraph. Do not include any cited information or evidence in the topic sentence. Use academic transitions like "first," "one reason," or "the most important reason" to help provide your essay with flow.*	
EVIDENCE SENTENCE **One to two sentences** *The evidence portion of your body paragraph is where you provide a cited quote or properly paraphrased information to support your thesis statement and topic sentence. It is important not to begin the sentence with a quote. Instead, provide contextual information about your evidence before providing it.*	
EXPLANATION **Two sentences** *In this part of the paragraph, explain how and why your piece of evidence relates to your topic sentence and helps to prove your thesis statement. Make sure you do more than rephrase your quote.*	
EVIDENCE SENTENCE **One to two sentences** *The evidence portion of your body paragraph is where you provide a cited quote or properly paraphrased information to support your thesis statement and topic sentence. It is important not to begin the sentence with a quote. Instead, provide contextual information about your evidence before providing it.*	

EXPLANATION **Two sentences** In this part of the paragraph, explain how and why your evidence relates to your topic sentence and helps prove your thesis statement. Make sure you do more than rephrase your quote.	

CONCLUSION

RESTATE YOUR THESIS **Two sentences** When you restate your thesis, make sure you are saying it in a different way without adding any new information.	
CONNECT TO LIFE **Two to three sentences** For the final part of your essay, connect it to life. What can society learn from your argument? How does the theme of the story still resonate today? Why are the issues you discuss still important? Where do we see the ideas you examine implemented today?	

If you are writing an argument essay, one of the body paragraphs will be set to include a counterargument:

BODY PARAGRAPH 3—THE COUNTERARGUMENT

TOPIC SENTENCE **One sentence** This sentence should address that not everyone agrees with your claim and that people have differing viewpoints.	
EVIDENCE SENTENCE FOR THE OTHER SIDE **One to two sentences** The evidence portion of the counterargument paragraph needs to address why people think differently. This piece of evidence should support an opposing viewpoint.	

EXPLANATION **Two sentences** *Now you'll need to explain why this evidence supports the opposing viewpoint.*	
FLIP THE SWITCH **One sentence** *Find and point out an error or a fallacy about this evidence and way of thinking. Flip the switch on the opposing argument and turn it upside down.*	
EVIDENCE SENTENCE FOR YOUR ARGUMENT **One to two sentences** *Now find a piece of evidence that supports your argument but also dispels the opposing side's reasoning. The more connected your evidence is to your argument, the better.*	
EXPLANATION **Two sentences** *Explain why this final piece of evidence proves your point and disproves the opposing side's argument.*	

At the beginning of a new school year, I set sentence-length requirements for each essay section for my students. Providing students with chunked sentence-length requirements helps students to focus on one task at a time.

Now, if students were to complete the outline above, they would essentially write their entire essays, and our class periods typically don't allow for that much independent writing time. So when I have my students complete their essay outlines in class, I require them only to complete their thesis statements and topic sentences, and provide all their pieces of evidence.

To avoid any confusion with this type of structured outline, especially if I am providing my students with a handout, I like to collapse the rows students *aren't* completing during the outlining process. This way, students fill out blank boxes on their outlines, but then they can also see that between these boxes they've completed, they will still need to go in and add more content to their essays later.

By completing those three portions of the essay outline, students will only have the hook, background information, and explanations to fill in independently. They will most likely also need to integrate their quotes and evidence into their writing seamlessly, but that is a skill we work on continuously throughout the entire school year. You can read more about how I work on fine-tuning students' writing in the next chapter.

Advanced Outlining

One of my goals when providing students with so much structure and support before they write their early essays is to eventually get students confident enough and capable of outlining their essays completely on their own. Eventually, as students have more practice outlining their writing, they can move from a more structured outline, like the one featured above, to an independent essay outline, like the one below.

This is a more advanced outlining style because even though it follows the same format as the guided outline, as mentioned above, the additional support and guidance are now gone. Students must rely on their previously learned knowledge of how to outline to complete an outline like the one below.

> **Teacher Tip:** To move from this more structured and formulaic outline, you can remove the numbered elements of the outline and have students outline only the Roman numerals. Once students have a strong foundation in writing, they will also know that they need to interweave their evidence, explanations, and analysis within each body paragraph.

I. Introduction
   1. Hook
   2. Background
   3. Thesis

II. Body Paragraph 1
   1. Topic Sentence
   2. Example
   3. Explanation
   4. Example
   5. Explanation

III. Body Paragraph 2
   1. Topic Sentence
   2. Example
   3. Explanation
   4. Example
   5. Explanation

IV. Body Paragraph 3
   1. Topic Sentence
   2. Example
   3. Explanation
   4. Example
   5. Explanation

V. Conclusion
   1. Restatement of Thesis
   2. Real-World Connection

> **Action Step:** Design the ideal essay outline for your students. Identify your writing prompt, essay requirements, and the elements you would like your students to outline.

What is your writing prompt?	
What type of essay will this be? (Argument or informational?)	
Is the essay structured or free-flowing?	
How many paragraphs will the essay have?	
How much evidence should students incorporate into their body paragraphs, and what types of evidence should they include? For example, must students include direct quotes, or is paraphrasing okay? Do you want to include a mix of both? If you are in doubt, start with less and build on those skills.	
Think about the purpose of each section of each paragraph. What skills do you want your students to practice for each essay section?	

As you work on writing in your classroom, think of every single essay as a part of teaching writing as a whole. The first formal essay should be more straightforward so students can focus on a few skills to start with. For example, for your first essay, have students include direct quotes (using sentence frames), and as the year progresses, move on to more advanced writing by having students include one direct quote and one paraphrased example for each body paragraph. This type of scaffolding will help students move from structured, formulaic writing to more free-flowing writing.

CHAPTER 5

The Three-Sentence Approach

As mentioned earlier in the chapter on planning backward, one of the units I changed was my short story unit. As I incorporated the elements of backward planning into my instructional design, I realized that I needed to start smaller—an entire paragraph was too much for the beginning of the year because I wanted to focus on teaching a few critical skills. Before I made the change, however, I had my students write entire paragraphs for each short story we read, and the students' skills got lost in the length of the assignment. Yes, they could write an entire paragraph, but to move on to more advanced writing skills, I needed to build my students' skills from the ground up.

For me to properly teach my students how to write an effective topic sentence that answers the prompt, how to embed evidence in their writing properly, and how to get away from writing "This quote shows," I needed to start small. I switched to three sentences. Because the writing assignment was much shorter, I could focus on specifically teaching those three skills, monitoring my students' progress, and reteaching the skills if necessary.

I made this switch several years ago—even before the pandemic. Rather than starting the semester with paragraphs or essays, I pared down my assignments to just the essential elements of a body paragraph and stopped there. I was left with only three sentences, and once I began my year focusing only on three sentences, I saw so much growth in my students. Not only did they understand the literary devices we were exploring and connect with the stories more, but they also became stronger, more confident writers.

The secret to this success is a combination of three teaching strategies: short writing assignments, sentence frames, and immediate feedback. Combined, these three teaching strategies provide students with the skills, practice, and reassurance that help them increase their writing efficacy, authentically learn how to write academically, and be more confident in their writing abilities.

In fact, my first two to four writing assignments for every new school year consist of just three sentences. I only move on to an entire paragraph once most of my students demonstrate a working knowledge of writing three sentences effectively. For my more advanced students who catch on earlier, I will find other ways to help them grow and challenge them as writers.

When introducing the three-sentence writing response, including multiple writing strategies (see chapter 1) in your instruction is essential. Specifically, I recommend using mentor texts, sentence frames, and color-coding to maximize effectiveness the first time you implement three-sentence writing responses in your classroom. When I introduce this approach in my classroom for the first time, I take an entire fifty-six-minute class period filled with revisiting our brainstorming from earlier in the week, reviewing sentence frames, sharing sentences in partner groups, and then writing and revising a response together. By dedicating this time at the beginning of the school year, students build a foundational understanding they can apply throughout the rest of the school year. However, it is never too late in the year to go back to the basics and implement this strategy, especially if your students are not grasping a writing skill. Likewise, it is also beneficial to revisit this skill throughout the year as well.

The Three-Sentence Response

DAILY LEARNING OBJECTIVE: Students will learn how to respond to a brief writing prompt with an effective topic sentence, a properly embedded quote, and an explanation sentence.

1. The Topic Sentence

For this strategy and for single-paragraph responses, the topic sentence is the first sentence of the response. An effective topic sentence introduces the idea and answers the prompt in one complete sentence. Mastering the topic sentence is an essential skill for students to learn on their way to becoming strong writers. They will also apply the same skills for their thesis statements and body paragraph topic sentences.

One of the acronyms I use for teaching students how to write a clear, concise topic sentence is GTAP: genre, title, author, and purpose. The four elements comprising the GTAP are crucial because each one is necessary for fully answering the entire writing prompt. I have my students use this acronym as a checklist for their writing assignments.

GENRE: What is the genre of the piece we are writing about? Establishing the genre of the text in which students are writing is important because it helps provide their writing with additional context.

TITLE: What is the title of the piece? This is a great opportunity to discuss the difference between placing titles in quotation marks for short stories and italicizing novels. It is also an excellent speaking point for pointing out correct title capitalization.

AUTHOR: Who wrote the piece? Again, this is a great sticking point for capitalizing proper nouns.

PURPOSE: What is the purpose of the writing prompt? This part of GTAP involves more than answering questions about the genre, title, and author, so I encourage my students to highlight and annotate the writing prompt.

2. The Quote Sentence

The "quote sentence" is the sentence containing the textual evidence. This is the sentence that contains the direct quote from the reading. These sentences are necessary for building strong writers because our students need to know how to include textual details—not just for their academic lives but for their lives outside of school. Being able to provide supporting evidence is a life skill.

For this part of the three-sentence writing response, it is essential to note that sixth-grader writing and tenth-grader writing capabilities will vary greatly. While I move my high schoolers away from quote lead-ins such as "The text says" and "In the text," those types of sentence starters for the quote sentence are much more developmentally appropriate for the middle school student.

It is essential to meet students where they are. As a high school English teacher, if my new students come in knowing they need to introduce a quote and not have it start a sentence, they are already ahead of the game. When I teach the quote sentence to my students, I teach these essential elements: indicator, lead-in, quote, and citation. These elements are necessary because otherwise, students will simply throw in a quote without any context. This format gives students a structure in which to embed their evidence.

INDICATOR: The indicator alerts the audience to an example.

LEAD-IN: The lead-in helps the writer seamlessly introduce the quote into their writing. For writing about fiction, the lead-in should contain information about the story that will help introduce the quote. For writing about nonfiction, the lead-in should introduce where the quote comes from and the context of the piece.

The Three-Sentence Approach

QUOTE: Only after the indicator and the lead-in do I have my students write their quotes. I encourage them to select a short part of the quote that is especially beneficial for their writing. I instruct them that the quote should be so essential that it has to be included as a direct quote rather than a paraphrased example.

CITATION: Finally, I instruct my students that all quotes need a citation followed by a period.

For even more explicit writing instructions for the quote or evidence sentence, refer back to the Academic Language Word Banks strategy in chapter 1.

Using color-coding and sentence frames to introduce the quote sentence are helpful strategies. Here is an example of a quote sentence I shared with my juniors during our *Into the Wild* essay.

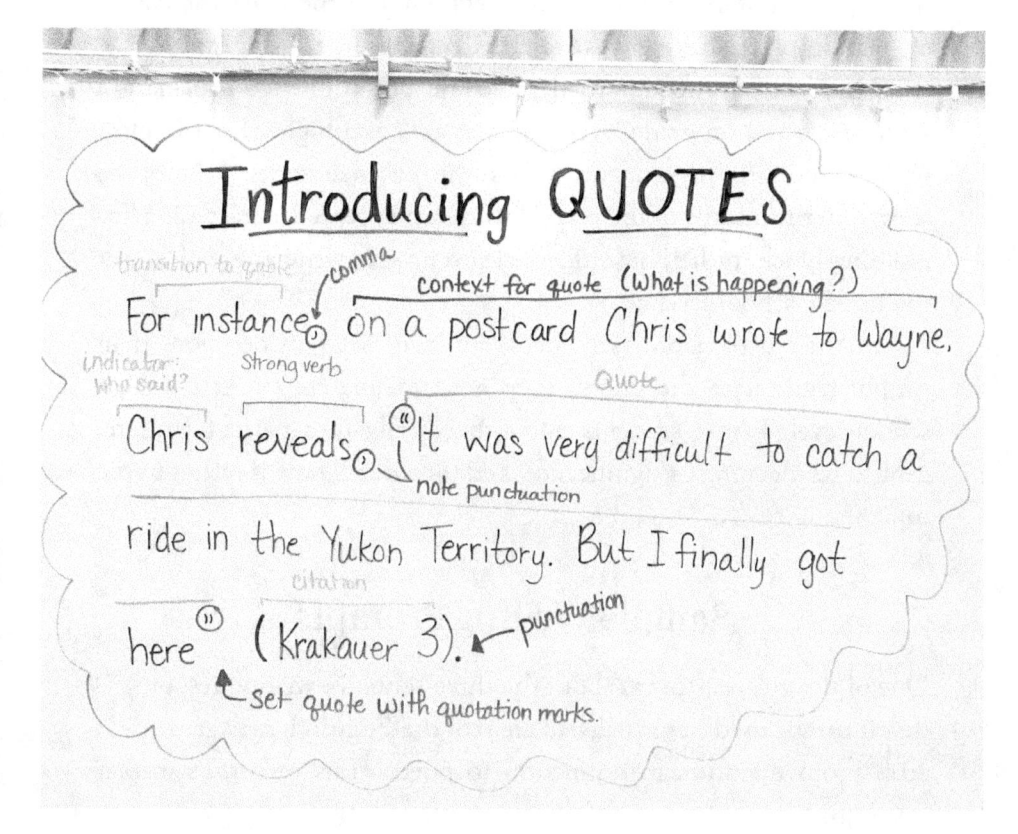

Introducing QUOTES

For instance, on a postcard Chris wrote to Wayne, Chris reveals, "It was very difficult to catch a ride in the Yukon Territory. But I finally got here" (Krakauer 3).

- transition to quote
- comma
- context for quote (what is happening?)
- indicator: who said?
- strong verb
- Quote
- note punctuation
- citation
- punctuation
- set quote with quotation marks.

If you examine this picture, you'll also see that I provided my students with a mentor sentence to introduce a quote. I broke that mentor sentence down and provided color-coded instruction and explanation for each part of the sentence.

3. The Explanation Sentence

An explanation sentence is a sentence in which a student provides additional explanation and analysis. This sentence should do more than simply restate the information from the quote. Once students become stronger writers, they will be able to offer additional analysis and explain how this evidence helps support and prove the topic sentence.

As always, make sure to scaffold your introduction to this concept. While at the high school level, I prefer at least two sentences of explanation, I only start with one at the beginning of the year. The goal is to start simply and expand as your students become stronger writers.

Again, be sure to differentiate your expectations for explanation sentences based on grade level. For example, as a high school English teacher, I cringe if my students still use the sentence starter, "This quote shows" in the middle of the year. However, that sentence starter is a key building block for helping students learn how to write academically at the middle school level.

In their explanation sentences, students need to do more than simply regurgitate the quote; they need to analyze it. At the high school level, I have students point specifically to a part of a quote, explain its meaning or significance, and then detail how it relates to the topic sentence.

Sample Writing Prompts

One of the greatest things about the three-sentence writing response is that it can be used in virtually all areas of the English language content area. From literature to nonfiction to poetry, this response's format is versatile.

Argumentative writing

- Do you agree with the author's assertion that XYZ? Provide textual evidence to support your answer.
- What is the best solution for XYZ? Include strong evidence to support your decision.
- What is the author's most important claim and why?
- What would the author of the text like the general population to do? How do we know this?

Nonfiction responses

- In three sentences, identify the author's main argument of the article and explain how the author develops the argument.
- Based on the information in the article, what conclusion can you draw about XYZ?
- What structure does the author use to convey their argument?

Literary analysis

- In three sentences, explain how the author uses foreshadowing to enhance the mood of the story.
- Based on the events in the story, what can you infer about XYZ's character?
- How does the author use setting to contribute to the story's mood?
- Where does the story take place, and how does the setting influence the events of the story?

CHAPTER 6

Reading Responses

One of the most vital skills we as ELA teachers hope to help our students develop is their ability to think critically about the world around them. One way we help our students build upon this skill is through the four pillars of the ELA framework: reading, writing, speaking, and listening. Everything we as English teachers do in our classrooms revolves around those four skills, and responding to stories and texts our students read in our classrooms is one way we help them hone their critical thinking skills.

The reading response is essential to our classroom because it supports reading comprehension, critical thinking, analysis, and writing skills. Assigning a reading response in class allows us to see where our students are. Did they understand the text? Are they able to analyze the text beyond basic comprehension? How do they apply their own diverse perspectives to the author's message? What is their takeaway from the story or text? The answer to those questions is where authentic learning stands.

However, not all of our students are ready for that level of comprehension, analysis, critical thinking, and writing at the beginning of the year. Before I incorporated this much scaffolding, intentional backward planning, and purposeful direct instruction in my classes, the writing responses that I would receive from my students were all over the place. They were off topic; they didn't answer the prompt, and I don't even think my students understood what they were supposed to be doing in the first place. Not only were my students' responses all over the place, but they also took me so much longer to grade because I had to sort through all of the responses that didn't even answer the prompt to assess the skills I wanted my students to demonstrate. These were all key symptoms of inadequate reading response passages.

Back then, I would follow along with my school's textbook: select a story, read the story, read the little comments in the margins, assign the questions at the end, and then have students write a response to the paragraph—and it was usually the prescribed prompt directly from the textbook. While I followed the book and the comments in the teacher edition, I wasn't specifically organizing my days to help my students succeed on the primary assessment piece: the writing.

By intentionally including backward planning and carefully selected strategies, we can guide our students from these inadequate responses to more meaningful writing and reflections. We can truly see their critical thinking skills alive in the words of their responses. We can help them think more critically about the stories and texts we read in class and the entire world around them.

Scaffolding Reading Responses

DAILY LEARNING OBJECTIVE: Students will learn how to write a response to literature by answering the prompt, providing evidence from the text, and connecting their evidence to the answer to the prompt.

Let's look at one of the very first academic writing prompts I assign my students. The prompt is about Kate Chopin's short story "The Story of an Hour." Students write about Chopin's use of symbolism and describe how it enhances her message or the themes of the story.

This is a challenging and high-level writing prompt I assign my students at the beginning of the school year, but they do not go at it alone. All week long as we work on the short story, I provide my students with scaffolds and brainstorming activities to help them be successful. I want them to feel ready and prepared for the writing assignment so they approach writing with an open, willing, and ready mind. Toward that end, I build students toward successful reading responses by following a five-step process:

1. Plan backward.

Before we look at the writing prompt and the process in which I use it in my classroom, I want to elaborate for a minute on all the preparation my students and I do to prepare for the writing prompt. I know that the end goal for the short story unit is to have my students respond to a literary analysis prompt that discusses and explains an author's use of a literary element and how it enhances the story's message.

As I examine my particular assignment, as described above, I think, "Okay, what do my students need to know?" First, they will need to understand and comprehend the story. They will also need to know what symbolism is, be able to identify symbols in the story, be able to explain what symbols stand for, find quotes or evidence of Chopin's use of symbolism in the story, identify the themes or the message of the story, and be able to embed evidence in their own writing in order to explain how it supports their answer to the prompt. Phew . . . that's a lot! But, by quickly checking all the skills my students will need to be successful, I lay the foundation for my instructional plans for the week.

2. Read the story and make sure students understand it.

Before we start reading our first short story, I teach my students about various literary elements and give them examples. Younger students may need more prep work about literary elements. However, even in my sophomore-level English class, the students still need a refresher on some of the most important literary elements: plot, conflict, foreshadowing, symbolism, setting, and more.

As a class, we read and discuss the story. I like starting with a short story, such as "The Story of an Hour," so we can read it multiple times, go through it and highlight key details, and discuss the story, all in a single class period. Once we do that, I like to have students identify some of the literary elements in the story to assess their understanding of literary elements quickly. I also use this identification to gauge their readiness to move on to the next step.

Here is my opening instructional slide for this day of instruction. In addition to some of the basic contextual information (author and date published), I also hook the students by letting them know this story was controversial. This immediately piques their interest, and it helps them analyze the story through a different lens. Furthermore, since I have already completed my backward planning, I direct my students' attention to critical features they'll be writing about—so I point out and even identify the key symbols.

"The Story of an Hour"

- Written by Kate Chopin in 1894.
- Examines the role women play in their own lives.
- Key symbols are heart disease and an open window -pay close attention to those.
- This story was **SUPER CONTROVERSIAL** in 1890. Why?

3. Do some group brainstorming.

I incorporate group brainstorming into almost all aspects of my writing instruction because it is an equalizer. There is a diverse mix of student abilities in my classrooms and in many other classrooms nationwide.

There are English learners in my classes and students with IEPs. While many of the strategies I employ in my teaching practice are geared toward these students, all learners in my classroom benefit from them.

With group brainstorming, I have students work together in small groups on either the entire part of the brainstorming task or just one portion. If students work collaboratively to brainstorm all the ideas needed to complete the writing assignment, the work can stay isolated to their groups. However, if students work collaboratively to brainstorm just one element of the essay, I have them share their ideas with the rest of the class by using activities such as informal presentations and posters, or moving around and sharing ideas with a new partner. Regardless of how group brainstorming is executed, the crucial aspect is to have the students take the lead in their learning and understanding of the prompt.

For my assignment on Chopin, I make students at each table responsible for going through the story again, but this time with the task of looking for a specific symbol. I assign the symbol of heart trouble to half of my students and the symbol of the open window to the other half. Each group of students is responsible for writing the symbol in the middle of a large piece of paper (11x17), finding and writing down as many quotes as possible relating to that symbol, and then discussing what they thought the symbol meant. At the end of this activity, each group should have an idea of what the symbol represents, and they will also have a plethora of quotes from the story specifically relating to their symbol. I keep these posters for future use so students can look back and refer to them on the designated writing day.

As you can see from this instructional slide, which I displayed during group brainstorming, I provided them with some information, but I had them complete the rest of the work by brainstorming ideas and evidence.

Symbolism in "The Story of an Hour"

Open Window	Heart Troubles
What does this symbolize? Find as many quotes for this symbol as you can!	What does this symbolize? Find as many quotes for this symbol as you can!

4. *Give direct instruction of a single, specific writing skill.*

Once students have brainstormed enough ideas, it is time to begin instruction for a specific writing skill. The first time I teach students how to embed quotes or evidence in their writing properly, I like to use a combination of mentor texts and sentence frames. By using mentor texts (preferably a teacher-written example from a previous story students are familiar with), students can see the final result and try to emulate it in their writing. By adding a sentence frame, students have the starting point for their own sentences. Gradually, students no longer need these scaffolds, but it helps them when learning a new skill.

If, for example, I plan on emphasizing properly embedding quotes for the first writing assignment, I will spend about half a class period using direct instruction and mentor texts to teach students how to embed a quote properly.

When I teach embedding quotes to my students, there are two key elements I have them focus on. First, I do not want them to start a sentence with a quote. Instead, I teach them to begin the sentence in their own writing and then add the quote into their writing. I inform them that they can do this by either writing a brief explanatory phrase or paraphrasing the beginning of the quote in their own words and then ending the sentence with the remaining portion. This is a skill that takes time and practice. The second element of embedding quotes successfully is that the quote should relate to the prompt's answer. Again, this skill takes time, but this is also where group brainstorming comes into play. After completing the group brainstorming, students should already have a variety of quotes to help them answer the prompt.

In their notes, I have my students write out the mentor text, highlight key portions, and label them. I also have them write out this formula, telling them that just like how in math they have formulas and equations that work to solve their problems, this word formula will do the same:

Intro the sentence in your own words, "quote" (cite).

For the word formula above, I have students highlight the "intro the sentence in your own words" in one color and label it. They also do the same for the comma, the quotation marks, the citation, and the period at the end. Throughout the school year, I have them refer back to these notes to help them write.

In addition to the direct instruction, notes, and mentor sentences, I also provide my students with sentence starters that they can use to help them properly embed a quote in their own writing. Here is a list of some sentence starters that are helpful for this process:

- At the beginning of the story when [explain what is happening], "quote" (cite).
- For example, after [explain an event that happened], "quote" (cite).
- To illustrate, toward the end of the story when [explain what is happening], "quote" (cite).
- In the story, [character name] says, "quote that is dialogue" (cite).

Usually, when I teach students about writing and assign the very first writing assignment of the school year, I hold off on using the

Academic Language Word Bank strategy (see chapter 1) for teaching students how to embed quotes. Before introducing that, I want to see where students are, focus on the topic sentence, and answer the prompt on the first assignment.

5. Use a sentence frame response.

After all that initial work, students are finally ready to begin their writing assignments. We rely on the tried-and-true three-sentence approach outlined in the previous chapter for that process. This approach works well for reading responses and literary analysis responses because it helps keep the writing simplistic while also focusing on key writing and analysis skills. To implement this strategy in your classroom, you will pair a simple writing prompt with a passage or short story and have a student respond. Since the students have only three sentences for writing, it is best to keep the prompt simple.

Here is what that looks like in the case of our Chopin example:

"The Story of an Hour" Three-Sentence Response

Prompt: In a three-sentence response, explain how Kate Chopin <u>uses symbolism</u> in her short story "The Story of an Hour" <u>to enhance the theme</u> or <u>give the audience a greater understanding</u> of the story.

Sentence 1: Include GTAP (genre, title, author's full name, purpose).
Sentence 2: Intro quote, "quote" (Chopin).
Sentence 3: Explain how the quote shows the purpose (enhance theme or understanding).

Response Title Goes Here

In the _____ "The Story of an Hour," author _____ uses _____ to symbolize _____ in order to _____. Intro quote in your own words and briefly explain what is happening in the story before the quote, "quote" (Chopin). (This use of symbolism enhances the theme because _____ / This use of symbolism gives the audience a greater understanding of the story because _____.)

When I share this sentence frame response with my students, I review the entire prompt and sentence frame with them, but then I break it down further—going sentence by sentence. Also, before we write the response, I ensure that students can access the group brainstorming they completed earlier in the week. On their group posters, students wrote down the symbol, its meaning, and several quotes from the story that show the symbol in use.

"The Story of an Hour" Writing Prompt

Sentence 1: Include GTAP (genre, title, author, purpose.)
Sentence 2: Intro quote, "quote" (Chopin).
Sentence 3: Explain how the quote shows the purpose (enhance theme or understanding).

"The Story of an Hour" Writing Prompt

SENTENCE 1

In the _____ "The Story of an Hour," author _____ uses _____ to symbolize _____ to _____.

Once students understand what will be expected of them for the three-sentence writing response, I have them all work on their writing, going one sentence at a time and starting with the topic sentence. As students write their first sentence, I circulate throughout the room to gauge how they are doing. When about 75 percent of my students are done, I ask a few students to volunteer and share their sentences aloud. This helps struggling students hear what their peers wrote and gives them ideas on what they can write themselves. Again, since this is the first writing assignment of the school year, it is more of a learning experience than an assignment.

"The Story of an Hour" Writing Prompt

SENTENCE 2

Intro quote in your own words and briefly explain what is happening in the story before the quote, "quote" (Chopin).

- For example, in the _____ of the story when _____, "quote" (Chopin).

Following peer sharing, we move on to the second sentence in the frame. At this point, I instruct students to refer to their group brainstorming posters. This is a prime example of how backward planning comes into play. When students have the quotes readily available, they can focus all their brain power on responding to the writing prompt rather than going back through the story and possibly getting distracted. With their evidence ready at hand and successfully embedded, students move on to the third sentence.

Before setting up this writing assignment, I knew the prompt and thought about what my students needed to know. I am setting my students up for success by scaffolding writing instruction this way.

They don't need to go back and look for a quote once they get here because they already have multiple quotes from which to choose.

> ## "The Story of an Hour" Writing Prompt
>
> **SENTENCE 3**
>
> Use just one of these sentence frames for your writing.
>
> - The use of this symbol proves that _____ because _____.
> - The use of this symbol illustrates _____ because _____.
> - The use of this symbol enhances _____ because_____.

After teaching my students how to formulate their responses using this three-sentence writing strategy, I give them the rest of the class time to write. This is typically a day where I am on my feet the entire class period, and after direct instruction, I check student work. Because this prompt is relatively simple, some of the students who are stronger writers complete this prompt quickly and finish before the end of the class period. When students finish, I invite them to check out my classroom library and read for pleasure.

When working with students struggling with literary analysis and writing, it is helpful to break up the instruction even more by briefly teaching students about sentence 1 (the topic sentence). Then give the students about five minutes to craft their own topic sentence. You will repeat this process for sentence 2 and sentence 3.

Exemplary Sample Student Response

You will know this strategy is working and that you have effectively and successfully implemented it when you notice several key elements in your students' writing. For starters, you will see your students respond to the prompt and write their topic sentence that includes the GTAP and fully addresses the question within the prompt. You will also see your students seamlessly embed their textual evidence into the response and provide an examination beyond a simple restatement of the quote. For example, in the sample exemplary student response below, you will notice that the student hit all the marks. Another sign of successfully implementing this writing strategy will be that your students will write with more detail and depth for each sentence. To illustrate, the student could have simply written, "In the short story, Kate Chopin uses symbolism to show the theme." And while that is a good start to literary analysis, it is missing so much compared to the sample topic sentence.

> In the short story "The Story of an Hour," author Kate Chopin uses the open window to symbolize Mrs. Mallard's desire to have freedom to enhance the theme of the story. For example, after Mrs. Mallard learns of her husband's death, she goes upstairs, looks out of an open window, and whispers to herself, "Free! Body and soul free!" (Chopin). This use of symbolism gives the audience a greater understanding of the story because it isn't until her husband dies that Mrs. Mallard truly feels free and happy.

While the response to this prompt could populate an entire multiparagraph essay, this sample response demonstrates multiple skills. First, the student knows how to address and answer a prompt. Second, this student demonstrates they can embed a quote properly and provide just enough context in their quote introduction for the quote to make sense. Finally, the student shows that they can write an explanation sentence that goes beyond retelling the contents of the quote by providing a deeper-level analysis of the quote and how the quote answers the prompt.

Now, at this point, you might be asking me, "Are you for real with this? You practically did the work for the student!" Or, you might also be thinking, "Really? You gave them an entire class period to write three sentences. My child, who is in fifth grade, could have done that!" Yes, I am for real, and yes, I give my students that much scaffolding at the beginning of the school year and dedicate an entire instructional day (fifty-six minutes) to this task.

It is important to remember that even though they have this sentence frame and the group brainstorming to rely upon, the students still do the heavy lifting. Furthermore, at the start of a new school year, not every student enters the classroom at the same level. Many students in my class need this much scaffolding and instruction to succeed on this prompt. With all this help, I am showing my students *how* to write academically but not telling them *what* to write in their responses.

Building Reading Responses

Once students understand how to write these three sentences academically, the next step in scaffolding the reading-response writing process is to add a fourth sentence—another sentence of explanation. By adding just one more sentence to my students' next writing task, I am still challenging them, but I am also gradually releasing the responsibility of writing an entire essay. These three- and four-sentence responses pack in a lot of high-level writing skills, and I want to make sure my students can focus on and learn these skills with a shorter prompt before moving on to an entire essay where they might be overwhelmed and forget to incorporate those skills.

When I add the fourth sentence to my students' writing assignments, I teach them more about commentary writing. I explain how the purpose of explanation or commentary writing is to explain how the evidence or quote they chose to include in their writing fully and completely answers the prompt. Regarding commentary writing, one of the biggest student writing mistakes I work on correcting in the classroom is helping students learn how to dig deeper and do more than simply restate what the quote says or use the phrase "this says" in their writing. The key to this writing strategy is to slowly build in more complex writing assignments for the students to complete so they can build upon their knowledge to become strong writers.

Once students have a solid foundation of responding in shortened paragraph responses (three to four sentences), then it is time to gradually release more responsibility to the students and build toward more complex, essay-length responses.

One of the first steps I take in increasing the length and rigor for my students is moving from those three-to-four-sentence responses I use at the beginning of the school year to a lengthier paragraph response that includes two or three inclusions of textual evidence. One of the biggest differences between the shorter paragraph response and the lengthier response is that the lengthier ones have more textual evidence. As mentioned before, this is a process. It takes time, and moving students from a three-sentence response to a multiparagraph essay takes time, practice, and patience.

After a few weeks of complete paragraph-length responses, you will most likely see that your students are grasping the major elements of response writing (answering the prompt in the topic sentence, seamlessly embedding evidence, and explaining the evidence in an analytical way). Once you do, you must graduate your students from the paragraph to the essay. Once again, starting small with a three- or four-paragraph essay is okay. It is best to spend a couple of days teaching students how to write an introductory paragraph complete with a thesis to move your students to a full-length essay.

Depending on what you prefer for hooks, explain to students what a hook or attention-getter for their essay is. In my classroom, I stick with an interesting detail, fact, or statement related to the author's message. (I find that far too often, students rely on questions as an "easy" way to begin their essay. If students are stuck on a question, a simple alternative is to have students rephrase that question into a statement!) Then, introduce students to the idea of background or contextual information. This is where I instruct students to include the GTAP from the three-sentence response. Finally, I teach the thesis statement. Use the color-coding strategy for thesis statements found in chapter 1 to help your students learn how to write a complete and effective thesis statement.

Once students write their first multiparagraph essay, they are ready for the next. The only real difference between a three-paragraph essay and a five-paragraph essay is the amount of supporting details and textual evidence. Yes, the length is different, but the skills are the same, and after progressing from three sentences to four sentences to a paragraph to a three-paragraph essay, your students are ready.

CHAPTER 7

Collaborative Writing

I remember the first time I assigned a collaborative writing assignment; it was out of desperation more than anything else. I was back at work for a new school year, and I had a three-year-old and a new baby at home. I was tired. I was exhausted. I was sleep-deprived and a full-time working mother in the classroom. On top of managing two children instead of just one, using my prep period and lunchtime to express milk, and having a baby with reflux issues (read: lots of crying, lots of waking up in the middle of the night, constantly needing and wanting to be held), I was teaching full-time. It was almost too much!

It was a lot, and I desperately needed a solution, so I decided to give partner essays a chance. At the time, I reasoned that assigning collaborative writing would cut my grading load in half and provide me with the much-needed time I sought. I was desperate to take work off my plate, and I needed to find a way to balance my career with my new normal at home.

I was so worn down that I blocked out any preconceived notions about collaborative writing. I suppressed my belief that I was cheating my students and that I wouldn't be giving them an opportunity to learn and grow as writers. As I went over the assignment and my students' eyes lit up at the idea of a partner essay rather than an individual assignment, I tried to ignore that nagging feeling deep inside me, telling me I was turning to collaborative writing assignments purely out of laziness.

However, as soon as my students chose their partners and began working on their essays, I started to see the benefit of collaborative writing. All of my previously conceived ideas about a partner essay were utterly wrong! I would have less to grade, but as I observed my students' work, I realized they were gaining so much more from the activity than I thought they ever would have.

I was amazed as I circulated throughout the classroom on the first essay-writing workday. Not only were students engaged in their work, but they were also having academic conversations about writing amongst themselves. They were brainstorming aloud. They were drafting their first few sentences in conversation and then revising them before they even wrote them down. As I walked around, what I heard was music to my ears. My students were engaged and talking about the writing:

> "How does this sound for our topic sentence?"
>
> "No, I think if you say this first, the introduction will be stronger."
>
> "We need to find a better quote for this paragraph because this one is kinda odd."
>
> "That sounds a bit off. I think we need to change this sentence."

Now, when I assign collaborative writing in my classroom, I don't necessarily do so to lower how many essays I will have to grade (although that is a major bonus); I assign collaborative writing so students have the opportunity to work through the writing process together with their peers. I've shifted my view on collaborative writing and view it more as a process of understanding rather than a summative assignment. Collaborative writing provides students with an opportunity for built-in editing and self-reflection with their peers. While it isn't always ideal as a way to assess individual student understanding, it is an ideal classroom activity for students to practice their skills. Even more beneficial is that collaborative writing assignments and activities fit in perfectly with the gradual release method.

Collaborative writing assignments function well as a way to gradually release the responsibilities of responding to a specified prompt once you've supplied adequate scaffolding and structure earlier in the school year. On the surface, collaborative writing activities are great because they give students an engaging group activity that helps reduce your grading load. More than this, though, collaborative writing exercises help struggling writers as they begin to demonstrate their new understanding of academic writing. Working in a small collaborative group, students experience a more sheltered setting as they learn to write academically. Furthermore, Dartmouth College affirms the benefits of collaborative writing in the classroom, stating that collaborative writing assignments (from peer review to collaborative papers) are essential parts of its writing classrooms at the collegiate level because "they encourage active learning, giving students the opportunity to become more deeply engaged with their writing, and with one another" (Dartmouth College, "Collaborative Learning/Learning with Peers | Writing," n.d.).

Through my experience, I've noticed three major benefits of including collaborative writing activities in your classroom:

1. Built-in Peer Editing

Because of the collaborative nature of group writing assignments, as students work on composing their shared assignment, they work through the writing process aloud, sharing and discussing the ideas they want to put on their paper. With each sentence that makes it on the paper, the group talks through the process of brainstorming, drafting, editing, and revising before deciding on a final, complete sentence.

When students work together to produce one well-written piece of writing, they incorporate each other's best ideas into the final piece. Not only do students have two (or more) sets of eyes looking at their writing, but they also draft and revise as they go.

2. More Individualized Instruction and Feedback

When you facilitate group writing assignments in the classroom, you have less grading. With less time dedicated to grading work, you can provide more specific and immediate feedback, which will then help the students grow as writers.

However, a collaborative writing activity is more of a shared learning experience than a summative assessment. So, rather than assigning grades for the final products, providing a complete or incomplete score and detailed feedback is best. What did students do that really worked? What is the strongest part of their writing? Why? How could students improve their writing? Which one or two sentences or which one paragraph can the students revise to make the composition stronger? The repetition of working together and receiving immediate and specific feedback will help students build self-efficacy to become more confident in their writing abilities, even when they are working independently. While this level of feedback is still possible and necessary for individual writing assignments, collaborative writing assignments reduce the total number of essays to grade, allowing educators to provide feedback immediately or in a much quicker manner.

3. Collaborative Learning

Studies have shown that one of the best ways to learn a concept is to teach it, and by providing students with the opportunity to write a paragraph or an essay together collaboratively, you transfer the responsibility for teaching to your students. Because peer writing assignments are collaborative, students act as both educators and learners as they work toward completing an assignment. Assigning a collaborative writing assignment is thus a great way to help students learn from their peers. Not only will students benefit from learning from one another, but they will also learn how to problem solve and work together in a group. For example, if two students disagree about how to transition from one sentence to the next and think their suggestion is the best for the final product, they will have to work together to come to a solution.

Not only are collaborative writing assignments beneficial for the students, they are also fun and engaging. Some of my favorite classroom days occur when my students work on collaborative writing activities. As my students are engaged in the activity, I can walk throughout the classroom to monitor how students are doing. I look for which students are leading the group, which students provide thoughtful feedback, and which students are passive observers.

It is important to note that the passive observers might not be disengaged. By nature, collaborative writing activities are a shared learning experience. By listening to the conversation and observing the process, the student who passively observes the activity also benefits from the activity. Academic research and practice also underscore the importance of collaborative writing activities for second language learners. Participating in collaborative writing activities is especially helpful for English language learners as they navigate their path toward biliteracy and learning academic language in a second language (Gibbons 2002, 129–131).

In addition to the help students receive from their peers through a collaborative classroom writing activity, peer writing is also extremely beneficial for adding strategies and scaffolding. To illustrate, when I am first teaching my students to write a complete paragraph response after reading a short story, I incorporate sentence frames and color-coding into the classroom activity. Since students are working together, not only do they focus on each element of the paragraph, but they are also reviewing each element their peers write, so they are both actively participating in writing and reviewing, which strengthens their skills as strong writers. For example, I like to use color-coding as one strategy to help my students learn how to write effectively. While I might use the color-coding strategy as part of a direct instruction method, it is also advantageous to use these same strategies in collaborative writing activities. Students who work together will be able to see how their peers react and incorporate these strategies into their responses. The same would also go for other strategies, including sentence starters and word banks.

Getting Started with Collaborative Writing

One of the most critical steps in planning a successful collaborative writing activity is to set expectations with clear guidelines. For the first few times you work on peer writing, it is best to plan to be on your feet walking around, monitoring, and helping students.

Set clear expectations

- Establish what students should be doing during this time.
- Establish what students should not be doing at this time.
- Inform students of approximately how long this activity should take.
- Set expectations for how students should respond when they disagree.
- Establish student guidelines for groups that finish early.
- Provide students with an example to use for modeling.

Literary Analysis Collaborative Paragraph for a Short Story

DAILY LEARNING OBJECTIVE: Students will work collaboratively to write a literary analysis paragraph demonstrating their understanding of the story. Rather than having my students write individual literary analysis paragraphs during my short story unit, I have them work together in groups of four to write a collaborative paragraph using markers and chart paper. This approach prompts students to actively think and talk about each sentence before setting markers to paper. This type of self and peer editing is so helpful in building strong writers.

In addition to having students work together, I incorporate another strategy: color-coding alongside sentence frames. I color-code each sentence in the paragraph a certain color so it helps students slow down and focus on the paragraph one sentence at a time. Also, since students are working on this together (and usually as one of their first paragraph responses in my classroom), I also share sentence frames to help guide their writing and model academic writing. By assigning each sentence in the paragraph a different and set color, students have to really think about what they are going to write in each sentence and what the purpose of each sentence is.

I task students with using large paper and markers instead of computers or pencils for this activity so I can walk around and easily see their work from a distance. I do not have to hover over their shoulders or ask them for their paper to check for understanding as I work. Additionally, when hung up, chart papers turn into mentor paragraph posters we can use the next week.

Sample prompts for this activity

- Discuss how the author's use of foreshadowing helps contribute to the story's theme.
- Discuss how the author's use of suspense helps contribute to the story's conflict.

- Explain how the author's use of symbolism helps contribute to the story's theme.
- Discuss how the author uses characterization to solve a conflict in the story.
- Discuss how the setting of the story builds the story's suspense.

Sequencing hint: I built this activity into my instruction toward the beginning of the year. I planned it after my students had a few weeks of practice working on their three-sentence responses and before I assigned individual paragraphs to the students. This collaborative writing activity really helped my students bridge the gap from writing only three sentences to writing an entire paragraph because they worked together and talked throughout the process.

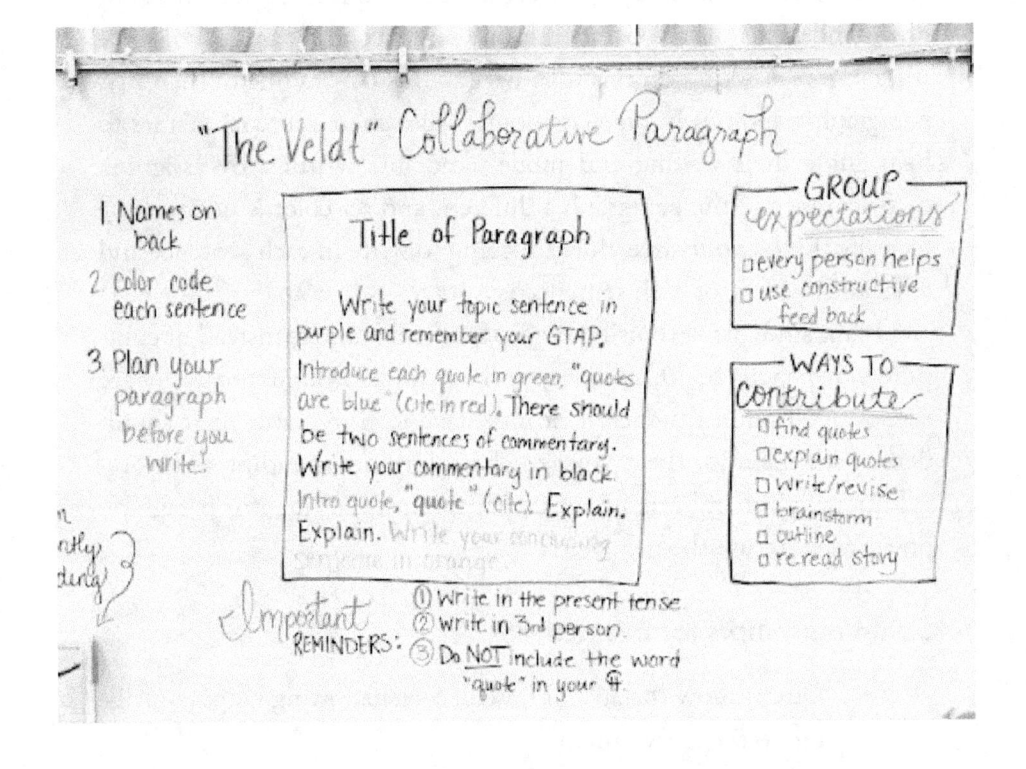

CHAPTER 8

Your First Formal Writing Unit

Let me paint you an all-too-familiar story that many teachers, including myself, experience at one point in their teaching careers. You've spent multiple weeks teaching your students small, focused writing skills. You've taught them how to answer a prompt, write a thesis statement, write a topic sentence, embed evidence in their writing, and even use academic transitions to connect their ideas. You've used multiple strategies to teach these skills, and students have even demonstrated their understanding of these skills to you through a series of small writing assignments here and there. You feel confident. You feel your students are ready to tackle a larger writing assignment, and so you assign a multiparagraph essay and let them have at it. After all, your class already showed you they've got it.

This is usually the point in time when students seem to completely forget all of their scaffolding, all of their strategies, and even all of their words. Many of the students in your class either produce an essay that is completely disorganized or completely off topic. And on top of that, they seem to have forgotten many of the skills and techniques you've taught them. As you sit there grading their essays that you felt so confident about, you ask yourself, "What went wrong?" After all, how could this have happened? The students were ready, but everything seemed to fall apart.

If this scenario doesn't sound familiar to you, consider yourself lucky. I've been in this situation multiple times, and it isn't a great place to be. In reality, many students might be completely overwhelmed with the task. Think about it. If you have a considerable number of items on your to-do list at work, at home, or elsewhere in your life, how do you feel? I know I can get overwhelmed pretty easily if I feel the tasks piling on and the time slipping away. The same is true for some of our students when we assign an entire essay.

One way to overcome, or even avoid, this scenario is to engage students in a fun, low-stakes writing assignment as an example to use during instruction, a hypothetical assignment if you will, about a topic that they love and know well before assigning an entire essay for the first time. I like to do this simultaneously as I assign the essay. I will divide my instructional time and use the low-stakes example assignment alongside direct instruction to help students learn the different aspects of essay writing. It is a means to teach writing an entire essay to my students. This low-stakes example makes independently drafting an entire essay more manageable while still focusing on those essential skills. Plus, the hypothetical prompt makes for a few really fun class periods! Bonus points if an administrator walks in on these days because even they will have a hard time not jumping in on the fun!

Teachers can help build students into confident writers by bridging that gap between what students love and are passionate about and writing academically for school. Yes, the two can coexist! I like to do this by using nonacademic topics for my sample essays, which I write alongside my students as they write their essays responding to an academic prompt. I use the same writing strands, but I engage students by making the connections between what they know and love and what I am asking them to do in my classroom. By doing so, I use fun, engaging, and safe topics to teach and model academic skills. I am making the art of writing fun for my students.

Writing about nonacademic topics is a crucial way to build stronger writers. While writing about something seemingly silly, like the best flavor of chewing gum, the most invincible superhero, or whether pineapple belongs on pizza, might seem like it lacks academic merit, the skills your students will use to produce nonacademic writing are actually quite academic. Students learn and use the skills they need while discussing topics they know and enjoy. After all, the standards say to write an informative essay that includes relevant and supporting details. The standards do not call for a specific, tricky academic topic. The goal is to employ the same strategies and scaffolds that students will use for their own academic writing, have students identify them in a context where they feel supported and safe (they know and like the comment so they won't be wrong), and then use those same skills and strategies on their own for all of the formal writing assignments they will encounter not just in your classroom, but in all other academic settings.

Many students claim they don't like reading. In reality, they enjoy reading but haven't found something they love reading. Similarly, with writing, many of our students might not have found a topic that they are passionate about writing about. Fostering a genuine love of writing is crucial in building our students up to be strong, capable, confident writers.

I Have Always Loved to Write

Not every student has an intrinsic love of writing. There are a few students in each class who genuinely love writing and who write outside of class, but as the years go on, that number seems to dwindle. Back when I was a teenager, I loved writing. I spent so much of my free time writing, and I looked forward to sitting down and writing.

I loved writing so much as a teenager that I self-published my own online teen zine via email during the height of the AOL days. When the idea first came to me, I eagerly ran to my family's one computer. I made sure nobody needed our single phone line, and I double-clicked on the AOL icon and logged into my account. Hearing the mechanical noises of the modem connecting me to the entire World Wide Web of possibilities filled me with excitement because I knew I was that much closer to writing and sharing my words with anyone who wanted to read them. Once I had a good number of subscribers, I set to work. Really, this is how I spent my spare time. I spent my downtime as a teenager writing and publishing articles.

I wrote, formatted, and published (read: typed, changed the font color, and emailed) a monthly teen zine. I wrote about anything and everything I loved and felt other teenagers would love as well. I wrote advice articles, how-to articles, and fashion articles. Looking back, I definitely wasn't an expert in any of these topics, but they were topics I loved and was passionate about, so I enjoyed writing about them. I would then format my email to make each article I wrote stand out. I would use a larger font size and bold my headline, and I would separate each article by using a different color. I loved every single moment of it.

Now, as an adult, I reflect on my earlier years and see that school and writing have always been an integral part of my life. I've always loved writing and school, so it is easy and enjoyable for me to write.

While some of our students love writing and truly have a passion and talent for it, that isn't the case for all of our students. Quite a few students are hesitant when it comes to writing about academic subjects. Perhaps they are doubting their knowledge on the subject or doubting their writing skills altogether. Whatever it may be, an essay can be a challenge for so many students. For so many students, even though they have brilliant ideas and are passionate about many things in their lives, their brilliance and hobbies might not translate well to academic writing in class. Or worse yet, previous experiences in a classroom setting have reaffirmed their own belief they are not good at writing. Now, I don't know about you, but if I believe that I am bad at something and I don't like to do it in the first place, I won't approach the task with an open mind and heart. I will begrudgingly do what I can, hoping my attempt at the task will suffice. This is why it is so important to go back to the basics and help all learners in our classrooms realize their true potential. This is why we need to start from the ground up, even if it means reteaching skills from several years back, to help our students view themselves in a new light.

Three Days to an Essay

DAILY LEARNING OBJECTIVE: Students will learn how to write an informative/argument/analytical/rhetorical essay by using mentor sentences from the whole-class essay example.

While prefacing formal writing assignments with a low-stakes alternative might seem time-intensive, the entire activity only needs to take three days of class time. Toward that end, I've broken the entire process down into three easy steps that can be folded in throughout a week of overall instruction.

Living and teaching in Southern California, I take many familiar things to my students and incorporate them into my writing instruction. From In-N-Out Burger to the Dodgers versus the Angels to the best beach locations, I hook my students in academic conversations about writing using topics they know and love. This helps generate excitement about writing, and it also helps increase class engagement.

Think about subjects your students are familiar with and love. They love TikTok. They love shoes and music. They love cartoons—the ones they watch now and the ones they watched in their younger days. They love food. They love to sleep. They love fashion. They love the world and care about their place in our world. You can use information about what your students know and love to make your writing instruction fun.

> **Action Step: Get to know your students and personalize your lesson to their interests.**
>
> | |
> |---|
> | What TV shows are my students watching right now? |
> | What hit movie are the students talking about? |
> | What's the newest trend that you see students participating in? |
> | What are many of your students' hobbies? |
> | What professional sports and athletes do your students follow? |
> | What fast-food restaurants do students in your area love? |
> | What are some of your students' biggest passions? Think about the social issues they care deeply about. |
>
> I like including topics that spark conversation, dialogue, and disagreement to add more engagement into these practice writing lessons. Once you better understand who your students are, what they do, and what they love, you'll have an easier time pulling them into the lesson.

Day 1: Prewriting activity

One of my favorite go-to writing instruction hooks is about food. More specifically, it is about In-N-Out. Being in SoCal, In-N-Out is a staple. Its crisscrossed palm trees are an iconic landmark, and its animal fries are a household name. I love In-N-Out and believe they make the perfect fast-food burger, but some of my students disagree. And when I say disagree, they adamantly disagree, and I love it because it sets the stage for the perfect discussion that naturally opens itself up to argument-based dialogue.

To begin our informal writing assignment, I write, "Who makes the best fast-food burger?" on the board. Then, I place a two-column chart drawn underneath the question. Students don't know it yet, but this is also an exercise in knowing the prompt and staying on topic: the specific question I ask my students is, "Who makes the best fast-food burger?" I don't ask them about fries, other side dishes, or milkshakes.

With the question on the board, I ask my students which one other chain restaurant we should pit against In-N-Out. They usually choose something like Shake Shack, the Habit Burger Grill, or Five Guys. For the sake of keeping things simple and also for time constraints, they can only choose one. I suggest taking a quick vote and choosing the most popular choice. In doing so, you'll get more classroom participation.

Once your class has decided on a contender, it is game on. (Oh, and by the way, only use In-N-Out as your first choice if you are on the West Coast. For this exercise, always start with a fan favorite in your region, whatever that may be.) Set a classroom timer for two or three minutes, and ask students to give you as many reasons as they can why place number 1—in this case, In-N-Out—is the best. To promote whole-class engagement, instruct students to share only one reason. Otherwise, you will have students sharing three or four reasons, preventing other students, and often quieter students, from sharing. In doing so, more students will have the opportunity to participate. When I do activities in the class like this, I like to call on the students who don't regularly participate in class first because I don't want their ideas shared by another student. This is a safe way to promote class engagement, especially with the students who are more reluctant to share. And I guarantee you, when you open up the classroom floor for discussion and debate about nonacademic topics such as this, you'll get more students involved and participating. It is a win all the way around!

As students share reasons why one place is the best, I like to add these reasons to the board using bullet points. In this way, the activity also builds on and models the brainstorming strategies students will use for their essays. At this point in the activity, I usually will have some students share ideas like "their French fries are the best" or "they have the best pink lemonade." This is when I gently remind them of the prompt and focus on the "fast-food burger" part of the prompt.

After a few minutes of students sharing reasons why place number one has the best fast-food burger, it is time to switch gears and spend the same amount of time on the second place. This is when I see students who have remained silent during the first part of the discussion jettison their hands up into the air because they are ready to defend their favorite burger. Just like with place one, students will share ideas as to why place two has the best fast-food burger, and I will write those down on the board. Sometimes, I like to call on a couple of student volunteers to write the information on the board.

Once students finish brainstorming ideas and reasons, I then use the information to form sample outlines, thesis statements, mentor sentences, and counterarguments throughout the essay writing unit.

I always have so much fun with my students during this activity, and it always makes me wish it was lunchtime. My students also have a lot of fun with this because even though they brainstorm ideas, classify information, organize topics, and engage in classroom conversation, the question is about something they love. I often have students leave the classroom at the end of the period, asking to do something like that again the next day!

Day 2: Drafting theses

Once students have completed the prewriting activity above as a group, we use the ideas they brainstormed during that activity as we move on to drafting.

1. Have students select the two or three strongest reasons from each category. For a five-paragraph essay, these reasons will eventually form the topics for each body paragraph.
2. Using those reasons, begin developing a sample thesis statement if you have not done so yet. (Read the teacher tip below to learn how you can incorporate this into an observed lesson.) I like to provide my students with a couple of different sample thesis options so they can select which format they prefer. Using more than one example thesis statement also shows students different ways to phrase their thesis statement.
3. As a group, discuss the example thesis statement. In particular, be sure to ask:
   - What is the main idea or topic of the writing?
   - What is the author's viewpoint or stance?
   - What details support this viewpoint?
4. Use color-coding to highlight how each part of the example thesis answers these questions and meets the needs of a solid thesis statement.

Color-coded sample thesis statements for an argument essay

Since this book is printed in black and white, please feel free to annotate these examples with colorful highlighters. In doing so, you'll see firsthand the true benefit of color-coding academic writing in the classroom. Similar to the strategies chapter (chapter 1), the text clues for each part of the thesis statement remain the same.

The main portion of the thesis statement that answers the prompt is underlined, and each supporting reason is indicated in either italic or bold text.

- While some people believe that [place 2] has <u>the best fast-food burger, it really is [place one]</u> because their burgers *have the best taste* and **quality ingredients**.
- <u>Even though [place 1] makes the best fast-food burger</u> because of its *superior taste* and **fresh ingredients**, there are some who say [place 2] is better because it offers more toppings.

Teacher Tip: If you know you've got an observation coming up and you'll be starting an essay within that time, this essay intro activity is great for classroom observations because administrators will see classroom engagement, direct instruction, and then student practice! If you are using this as an observation lesson, you can add to it and have students work in pairs to write sample thesis statements based on the information brainstormed. Student pairs would write a sample thesis statement, share it with another student pair, and then share the strongest statement from the two student groups with the class. Eventually, toward the end of the observed lesson, I suggest coming up with a sample thesis statement that you will then use in the writing instruction in the future.

Challenge: If your sample thesis statement is for an argument-based essay, as a challenge activity, you can ask students to write another sample thesis statement but for the opposing viewpoint. This challenge activity can be done individually, in pairs, or in small groups.

Day 3: Drafting topic sentences

Just like how I like to keep my sample thesis statements student-friendly in the beginning of the school year or for our first formal writing assignment, the same applies to my sample topic sentences. Think of it as building the framework. Once students know which basic elements they need to include in their topic sentences and demonstrate mastery of a simplistic topic sentence, they are ready to venture out and practice trying more advanced writing styles.

When I teach my students how to write topic sentences at the beginning of the school year, I find myself returning to the basics and building their skills from there. Many students already know how to write topic sentences, which is perfectly okay. If anything, the review reinforces what they know and helps improve their confidence because they enter the lesson knowing the content. I always encourage students who already feel confident to add to or make the sample sentence their own if they feel they are ready.

1. Identify and brainstorm academic language with your students that works for the specific prompt. For example, while it is simplistic, terms like "one reason, another reason, and the last reason" add organization and cohesiveness to an essay. Students might also say something like, "first, second, and third." I like to brainstorm quite a few of these with students so they have options to choose from and play around with.
2. Using the academic language you brainstorm with your students, begin developing sample topic sentences as a class.

Sample topic sentences

- One reason [place one] has the best burger is because their burgers have the best taste.
- To begin with, [place one] has the best burgers because their burgers have the best taste.

3. As with the sample thesis statement, identify how each section of the sample meets the needs of a good topic sentence. In particular, be sure to help students notice the following:
    - The topic sentence should begin with an academic transition.

- The topic sentence should respond to the prompt and state the paragraph's main idea.
- The topic sentence should include a supporting detail.
- Color-code the sample topic sentence accordingly.

4. The example topic sentences above are simple. Some students will want to write with a more colorful and expressive style, and once they demonstrate that they understand the concept, it is important to let them try.

Color-coded sample topic sentences

In these examples, the academic transitions are underlined, the main idea or answer to the prompt is in plain text, and the reason is bolded.

- <u>One reason why</u> [place one] has the best burger is because their burgers **have the best taste.**
- <u>To begin with</u>, [place one] has the best burgers because their burgers **have the best taste.**

> **Teacher Tip:** If you are pressed for time but still need to focus on direct writing instruction as your students write their own essays about a different topic, use the nonacademic essay example as a mini-lesson at the start of each class period. Plan your focus for the class periods to be whatever skill you are teaching and demonstrating for the sample essay.

Putting it all together

By having students write along with you as you work your way through the example essay topic, you model the writing process for the students, making writing a formal essay more accessible. If I am working on an argument essay with my students, I let them know from the beginning that they will need to explore multiple viewpoints in their essays and that they will need to have a counterargument. Once students write the thesis statement and their topic sentences, I apply the same strategy to demonstrate what a topic sentence for a counterargument paragraph should look like.

As you can see, I love using nonacademic topics as the jumping-off point for writing instruction. This type of introductory writing activity engages the student. It helps you create a safe space for writing and expression because students will feel more connected to and comfortable with the writing prompt. At the end of the class period, if a student learned how to write an effective thesis statement, does it matter if it is about shoes or Shakespeare? English class is very skills-based, so sometimes, one of the best things we can do for our students is to take a step back and focus solely on the skills.

> **Teacher Tip:** A great way to incorporate this teaching strategy into your classroom is to have the students write their essays concurrently with you as you use the nonacademic topic as an example. Using this fast-food burger essay as a teaching strategy and example text, students can see how to write an essay and then transfer that understanding to their topic and write using the same color-coding strategies. By doing this for the brainstorming, outline, sample thesis statement, and topic sentences, students will have enough instruction to begin tackling the writing assignment.

I've found that food and pop culture are some of the most engaging topics for this exercise, but here are other potential topics you could use to engage your students in writing instruction.

Informative essays

- What makes a good TikTok video?
- What elements are in every classic fairytale?
- What inventions have had a significant impact on society?
- What elements make a good theme park?

Argument essays

- Does pineapple belong on a pizza?
- Who is the worst/best animated villain?
- Who makes the best sneakers?
- IOS or Android?
- Do superheroes have to fly?
- What's the best superhero power?
- Sour or chocolate candy?
- What is the greatest animated movie of all time?

CHAPTER 9

Peer Editing

Peer editing is a crucial step in the writing process. Not only does peer editing help students learn to read essays with a critical eye and through the lens of an editor, but they also get exposure to their peers' writing, which helps them gauge how they are doing as writers themselves.

So often, I've heard from tired and frustrated teachers who have all but entirely given up on peer editing in the classroom because it just doesn't work. And I've been there. Looking back, the first time I assigned peer editing in my high school English class, I didn't know my expectations. I think I just assumed that my students would trade papers with one another and look over the essays carefully and critically, examining the paper for grammatical errors and ways to help their peers. I thought they would write comments in the margins about how their partner could improve their paper. I thought they would use their red pens to correct comma splices and misspelled words accurately. Again, I don't really know what I was thinking, and that was entirely evident when I tried to conduct the activity in the classroom.

The first time I ever conducted peer editing in my classroom as a first-year teacher, I magically hoped that each student would take the task seriously and actually know what to do. I had high expectations for my students, but I didn't realize that my expectations were completely unreasonable at the time. I didn't even teach my students how to read and correct like editors, yet I tasked them with just that. If I wanted my students to catch every run-on sentence, I first had to teach them about subjects, predicates, phrases, and clauses. Rather than giving them clear guidance, some instruction, and a checklist of areas to examine, I just set them free to attempt a task they weren't ready for.

Simply put, even though I didn't know what to expect, my expectations were too high, and my students were unprepared for the task of peer editing. I did not set my students up for success. In order to make peer editing successful in the secondary ELA classroom, there are two things we need to do. First, as teachers, we need to reframe our thinking and our expectations of peer editing. Second, we must teach our students how to peer edit to make the activity worthwhile in the classroom.

Peer editing needs to be understood as part of the writing process rather than the end of it. Peer editing should take place between the first draft and the revision process. Students need dedicated time in class to review their edits and suggestions and make any necessary changes before submitting their final drafts. Seeing those edits, reflecting on their writing, and adjusting their work is where real, authentic learning happens. Unlike mathematical equations, which have a clearly defined start and endpoint and one correct answer, there is always room to edit and revise one's writing. Teachers should not view peer editing as a means to an end in students' writing. After peer editing, a student's paper won't be perfect, nor will it be completely finished. However, when it comes to peer editing, we should focus on the process and not the final result.

In years past, when I had my students complete their first formal essay of the school year, I noticed a shift in how students viewed peer editing. They were looking at the end product as the goal. They only seemed to care about how the process improved their paper because they wanted to receive the highest grade possible. While they were focused on the endpoint, they should have focused on the process of peer editing and how the act of peer editing made them a stronger writer. It's about more than just the final draft.

The sole purpose of peer editing is not for students to completely free their papers from grammatical errors. Instead, the goal of peer editing should be to help students become stronger writers by getting them to read, think, and write like editors.

When I introduce peer editing to my students, I emphasize that their work will not be perfect even after peer editing. I ask them to think about published writers with teams of editors, and I underscore that there are still errors in published works—even works reviewed by professionals. So I tell my students that the goal is to use the peer editing process to become stronger writers themselves. I tell them that after the activity, I want them to look at their papers with a new perspective. I tell them that I want them to keep peer editing in mind for future essays they write. I tell them that a stronger essay is just the byproduct of the process.

Like all writing skills, peer editing requires explicit instruction and scaffolding, plain and simple. Similar to how we would completely overwhelm ourselves and our students if we attempted to teach and assess all of the aspects of writing with every writing assignment, the same holds true for peer editing. If we expect our students to catch every single error in their peers' writing, we are setting them up to fail. Rather than having students simply exchange papers and start peer editing, we first need to teach our students how to read like editors and what our expectations are.

Scaffolding Peer Editing

DAILY LEARNING OBJECTIVE: Students will learn how to read and think like editors while participating in a peer editing activity.

When introducing students to peer editing, it is best to start small and provide students with examples of how to complete the peer editing. In my classroom, I like to utilize peer editing checklists to help guide students through the peer editing process. For them to be successful, they need guidance along the way, and checklists meet that need. Here is what a peer editing checklist might look like toward the end of the school year after students have had ample classroom practice with various parts of the essay:

Peer Editing Checklist

DIRECTIONS: For each part of the peer editing checklist, indicate "yes" or "no" on the line to inform the author about their paper's progress. For the last two questions of each section, provide your author with specific information on what they did well and how they can improve their paper.

Introduction

- Does the author include the GTAP (genre, title, author, and purpose) in the introduction?
- Does the author include adequate background information in the introduction to introduce the audience to the topic?
- What is one thing the author does well in the introduction?
- What is one thing the author can do to improve the introduction?

Body paragraphs

- Does the author begin each body paragraph with a topic sentence?
- Does the author include evidence in the body paragraphs?
- Is the evidence properly introduced, quoted, and cited?

- Does the author explain how the evidence helps prove the topic sentence and thesis statement?
- What is one thing the author does well in the body paragraphs?
- What is one thing the author can do to improve the body paragraphs?

Conclusion

- Does the author restate the thesis statement?
- Does the author avoid adding in any new information?
- Does the author connect the essay to life or to the message of the story?
- What is one thing the author does well in the conclusion?
- What is one thing the author can do to improve the conclusion?

Grammar and conventions

- Does the author include proper capitalization?
- Does the author maintain a third-person perspective throughout the essay?

To help students succeed with peer editing, they must have sufficient knowledge of what they are checking for. For this sample peer editing form, I would first make sure my students saw examples of properly embedded quotes, proper capitalization, and third-person writing. Furthermore, since this is a multiparagraph peer editing checklist, I know I've already spent sufficient time teaching my students how to write a paragraph and how to properly include evidence in their writing.

> **Action Step: Plan your peer editing checklist.**
>
> | | |
> |---|---|
> | What is the writing prompt? | |
> | List the specific writing skills you focused on for this unit. | |
> | What four things would you like your students to check for during peer editing? | |
>
> A helpful tip for creating an effective peer editing checklist for your writing assignment is to start small. As the year progresses, add more skills to the checklist, but at the beginning of the school year, focus on fewer elements to help students master those skills—both in writing and editing.

Knowing how important it is to start small and focus only on a few elements at a time, especially at the beginning of the school year, here is what the checklist might first look like when students are only writing a paragraph:

Paragraph Peer Editing Checklist

DIRECTIONS: For each part of the peer editing checklist, indicate "yes" or "no" on the line to inform the author about their paper's progress. For the last two questions of each section, provide your author with specific information on what they did well and how they can improve their paper.

Paragraph

- Does the author include the GTAP (genre, title, author, and purpose) in the introduction?
- Does the author include two pieces of evidence?
- Does the author answer the prompt?

- What is one thing the author does well in the paragraph?
- What is one thing the author can do to improve the paragraph?

Another way to help scaffold the process of peer editing in the classroom is to have students participate in small group or partner gallery walks. When I have my students write a collaborative paragraph, I like to follow up the collaborative writing activity with a gallery walk where students are tasked with reading and providing feedback on at least three other paragraphs. This way, students can learn to critically read and provide feedback on their peers' work in a group setting. Plus, it helps generate dialogue and discussion about writing, improving writing, what the students did well, and what the students can do to improve their writing.

When students complete a gallery walk, I provide them with a simple chart to complete (both for accountability and as an introduction to peer editing). Here is what the chart might look like for a paragraph:

Paragraph Writing Gallery Walk Observations

DIRECTIONS: Read and comment on three different paragraphs. Make sure you fully answer every question in each column.

#	Topic Sentence	Quotes	Commentary	Overall
	Does the topic sentence include the GTAP? Does it answer the prompt?	Were they properly introduced and cited? How do the quotes help answer the prompt?	Did the commentary connect the evidence to the topic sentence? How else could you connect the commentary to the quote and topic sentence?	What is one thing the group did well? How could the group improve?

Peer editing can be a powerful and beneficial activity in the classroom if we manage our expectations for the activity and provide students with a solid framework to work with.

There are many indicators of successful and effective classroom peer editing. As a classroom teacher, you will know if your students benefited from the process based on your visual and auditory observations during and after the peer editing session. During the peer editing session, one of the biggest indicators of success is when a student calls you over to confer with you about something in their peer's writing. They might think they've found a mistake or have a way to improve the writing, and they want to check with you before suggesting it to the student. When students reach out to their teachers for help during peer review, it is a clear sign that they are taking the activity seriously, want to do a good job on it, and are thinking like editors. I always make sure I circulate throughout my classroom during peer editing so I am available to my students to reach out if they need to.

Another sign of a successful peer editing session you might see midsession is when students reach out to one another for clarity about something one of them wrote. This action shows that the writing might not have been entirely clear, and so with a quick and impromptu student-to-student conference, both parties involved can work together to improve the sentence or paragraph. As teachers, we might feel a little frustrated if this happens, but in reality, it proves that the students are striving to complete peer editing to the best of their abilities.

Finally, teachers will also be able to tell if the peer editing session was successful based on those first few moments in class once students switch their papers back to their original owners. Once this happens, if your students are reading the edits, making notes on their document or paper, and conferring with students about why they made suggestions, it was a successful and effective peer editing session.

While, in an ideal world, peer editing would magically fix every single error in student papers, it is so important to remember that perfection is not and won't ever be the goal for student writing. The goal is to see growth in the process and for students to work toward becoming strong writers.

CHAPTER 10

The First Five Minutes of Class

Bell ringers, do nows, daily warm-ups, independent reading time, or sit down and please get something out—whatever you call it. Those first five to ten minutes of class time are crucial for setting the tone of the class period, warming students up for learning your content, and starting out the lesson.

I am an adamant believer in having a steady, consistent routine for starting class, which is a daily bell-ringer activity for me in my classroom. Having an independent activity planned for the first five to ten minutes of class is how I settle into one class period while transitioning from the previous one. I use that time to take attendance (and with thirty-five students, taking attendance in a timely manner can be a task in itself), greet students, answer individual student questions, and check in with students who seem a little dysregulated. It takes some up-front work at the start of the new school year to get students into the routine of starting the bell ringer or warm-up immediately when the bell rings, but once everyone gets on board, ultimately that regularity helps free up those crucial moments at the start of the period.

However, having a dedicated time to enter my attendance and say, "Hey, how is your day going?" to most of my students isn't the main reason why I assign work at the beginning of the period. Bell-ringer work is also beneficial because I like to use it as a quick way to engage my students in the lesson, especially if we are in the middle of a writing unit. When I am giving explicit writing instruction or when my students are working on a larger writing assignment, I get the students started each period with a small, quick, manageable task that will help them accomplish the day's learning objective.

There are quite a few different kinds of bell ringers or warm-up exercises you can do in the classroom to build your students into strong writers. Some warm-up writing exercises are more generic and focus more on skills than content, and others are more content-specific and geared toward a specific writing assignment. Let's take a look at both kinds of writing warm-up exercises.

Generic Writing Warm-ups to Build Strong Writers

Sentence combining

I absolutely love it when I assign my students a sentence-combining activity! Sentence combining is an engaging and exciting way to show students the power of language and the written word.

You share three to five simple, yet related sentences with your students for this activity. Instruct students to combine those sentences into one complex or compound-complex sentence without changing the integrity or meaning of any of the sentences. Students can omit words. Students can add words. Students can rearrange how the information is written. The only thing students cannot do is change the meaning of the original sentences.

This activity doesn't necessarily have to be related to your teaching content. The key skill here that students practice is syntax. They actively read and analyze the cluster of simple sentences. They actively think about how to combine that information into the best sentence possible with correct punctuation. From there, students write out their sentences. I like to take this activity one step further by having my students volunteer to share and read aloud their combined sentences with the punctuation. By hearing their peers read their sentences aloud, students realize there are many different ways to say something, and that writing is a very powerful and beautiful skill.

I even like to push my students to the next level with little challenges once they get used to this warm-up. I'll ask them to write their combined sentence in two different ways, or I'll ask them to write the sentence using as few words as possible or to write the sentence correctly using a semicolon. The possibilities for these challenges are endless, and they provide students with a safe, accessible way to spread their writing wings and try something new.

Sample sentence combining activity

DIRECTIONS: Combine the simple sentences into complex or compound-complex sentences that do not change the meaning of the original sentences while using proper grammar and punctuation.

Simple sentences to share with students

1. The cat was small.
2. The cat was orange.
3. The cat chased a duck on a sunny day.
4. The chase happened in a field.
5. The duck was yellow.

Possible student responses

1. A small orange cat chased a yellow duck in a field on a sunny day.
2. On a sunny day, the small orange cat chased the yellow duck in a field.

3. In a field on a sunny day, the orange cat chased the yellow duck.

The most essential thing for this writing warm-up is to ensure that students do not change or alter the original meaning of the sentences. If students can do this and see how they can use the words to convey a message, how they can interchange the words, and how they have freedom in doing so, they will gain confidence in their writing skills.

Fixing grammatical errors

I'm not sure about you, but when I see flagrant grammatical errors in the wild, I first think, "Oh, man, that's bad," and then I like to share them with my students to see if they can catch and correct the errors. There are so many places to find grammatical errors in the wild to share with your students. A quick web search will turn up social media posts, billboards, and even advertisements with obvious, and even funny, grammatical errors.

A quick and easy way to turn your students into copy editors and get them thinking like editors is to share these writing errors with them. Inform students that you are sharing something with them that has an error and ask them to work independently or with partners to find and correct them. I even like to add extra student kudos if they can explain what is wrong with the error.

Sample Fixing Grammatical Errors Activity

DIRECTIONS: Look at and analyze the image. Find the grammatical errors, be able to explain why each error is problematic, and rewrite the sentence or phrase using correct grammar and punctuation.

Image to share with students

[A caution sign reading "CAUTION PEDESTRIANS SLIPPERY WHEN WET"]

Sample student responses

- Attention Pedestrians! This surface is slippery when wet.
- Pedestrians, caution! This area is slippery when wet.

These search terms will help you locate pictures with grammar errors in the wild:

1. Grammar errors in real life
2. Grammatical errors on billboards
3. Social media posts with bad grammar
4. Spelling errors on billboards
5. Punctuation errors in real life
6. Punctuation errors on signs
7. Funny grammatical errors

Once students demonstrate that they can handle the activity, identify and correct the error, and have a quick classroom conversation about it, let them have fun.

Short mentor texts

Another way to warm up your students and prep them for writing is to give them a mentor sentence or a brief mentor passage. I identify one specific element the author did exceptionally well, and then ask the students to write a sentence or brief passage about any topic of their choice (school appropriate, of course), modeling that sentence and re-creating what the author did well. You can have them model the sentence structure, the punctuation usage, or the depth of imagery.

Try to find mentor texts that are one to three sentences long. Any longer than three sentences will get challenging during the time constraints of the first five or ten minutes of class.

Sample Mentor Text Activity

DIRECTIONS: Look at and analyze the quote. Use the quote as a mentor text and re-create the sentence using a topic of your choice that mirrors the mentor text.

> *Beauty is an enormous, unmerited gift given randomly, stupidly.*
> — KHALED HOSSEINI

For this mentor text, have students look at and analyze the punctuation, specifically the comma between the two adjectives and two adverbs. Then, have students create a similar sentence that includes two adjectives and two adverbs to describe something and what it does. This intentional focus on dual modifiers will help students learn how to use commas correctly to be more descriptive and vivid in their writing.

> *Darkness cannot drive out darkness; only light can do that. Hate cannot drive out hate; only love can do that.*
> — DR. MARTIN LUTHER KING, JR.

For this mentor text, have students look at how Dr. Martin Luther King, Jr., uses multiple examples of juxtaposition—darkness and light, and hate and love—to emphasize his message. Encourage students to brainstorm juxtaposing ideas for their sentences to enhance what they are saying.

CHAPTER 11

Empowering Strong Writers

In addition to building classroom community, facilitating a positive classroom culture, and spending time with my students (who, by the way, make me smile, laugh, cringe, and think, "What in the world is going through your mind?" about a hundred times a day), teaching writing is one of the aspects of my job that I am most passionate about. It makes me sad to know how many students enter their ELA or English classrooms completely dreading and hating writing. So many students have this preconceived notion stuck in their minds that they are terrible writers and hate writing, which isn't true at all. I can't even tell you how many times I've had a student ask me to look over their paragraph, essay, or even college-admittance essay for advice, and before I finish reading their first sentence, they tell me, "I'm not a good writer." It just makes my heart heavy that our students, even our high school seniors, who are still babies, already think so poorly about their writing skills.

Students' low self-esteem and self-efficacy about their writing abilities not only hold them back from growing to their true potential but also prevent them from trying, taking risks, and truly being able to grow as writers. That is why I teach writing the way I do. That is why

I start from such a basic and simple level with even my high school students. That is why I provide my students with so many scaffolds and supports throughout the entire class year, but most importantly, at the start of a new school year. I never want one of my students to think they are a bad writer or not smart enough to answer the prompt. I want to give them all the necessary tools to grow as writers and flourish in my classroom and all areas of their lives where writing will come into play.

If you've hesitated to provide your students with this much support before, that is entirely okay. Teachers face so many pressures from the administration, other teachers, parents, the community in which we serve, and more, that sometimes going against the grain (even if you know it will benefit the students) can be almost too much to think about. Before I started teaching with more scaffolds, more differentiation, and more strategies, I had plenty of reservations myself. In my earlier teaching days, I could have even told you I was too afraid of dumbing down the curriculum, or that I already graduated from high school and my students needed to do the work, not me. I could have told you that students should be able to sit down during class and write an academic paragraph. I also could have told you that color-coding is basic and doesn't belong in high school, and especially not in a twelfth-grade classroom.

This old-fashioned way of thinking and outdated way of teaching is antiquated. It does not resonate with or help most students in our classrooms today. The learners in our classrooms, the students, the children we see day in and day out, are not a homogeneous group of students coming to us with the same knowledge, skill set, and understanding of the language. Our students, the kids we teach, come to us from all backgrounds, abilities, and knowledge levels, and many are not at grade level.

If we were to look only at the state or national standards for the grade levels in which we teach and deliver our instruction, curriculum, activities, assignments, and lessons only to students who are at that level, we would be leaving out so many of our learners who would benefit from slowing down, going back to the basics, and teaching (and assessing) just a few writing skills at a time. If we make the time in our pacing guides to accommodate students who need extra support and scaffolds, we would truly build up all our students from the foundational level into strong, confident writers.

If you think you are taking it too easy on your students by providing them with too many instructional strategies for teaching writing, please know that you are genuinely helping the majority of the students in your classroom. Long gone should be the days when teachers assign writing to students and assess the students' writing without first spending adequate time teaching writing skills. Before we send students off to write independently and assess their writing, we first need to fully break down every part of the writing process—not only teaching students how to write academically but also making sure students have a basic understanding of the fundamental skills from previous grade levels.

There is nothing more frustrating for a student who comes into a classroom already struggling as a writer (whether it be a language acquisition issue, a gap in content knowledge, or lack of skill mastery from several grades back) and then being assessed and earning a poor score on a skill the current teacher did not specifically teach or review. A little review of the basics goes a long way. And yes, you better believe it: with my strategies, I show my sophomores how to capitalize the title of a short story and punctuate the end of a sentence. Yes, these are things they should know. But if I have just one student who comes to my classroom without this knowledge, for whatever reason it is, I do not want to discourage or ostracize that child or make them feel inferior because of a lack of skills or knowledge.

So, the next time you set out to teach, assign, and assess writing, I want you to feel empowered. Feel empowered to slow down. Feel empowered to go back to the basics, however elementary and fundamental those basics may seem. Feel empowered using multiple writing strategies with your students. Feel empowered to provide your students, even if they are seniors in high school, with sentence frames and sentence starters. Feel empowered showing students how amazing writing can be. Feel empowered to show them the power of the mighty word.

Feel empowered to build your students into the strong writers they are destined to be.

Acknowledgments

To Dave Burgess, Tara Martin, and the entire DBI team, thank you for believing in me and for believing in this book. Thank you for providing me with the opportunity to share my love and passion for teaching writing with so many more people.

To my editorial director, Lindsey Alexander, and her editorial team, thank you for the support and constant communication once I submitted my initial manuscript.

To my husband, I love you. Your support, love, and encouragement mean the world to me. Thank you for always believing in me and helping me reach my dreams. Thank you for being a wonderful husband and even better father. I would not be where I am today if it were not for you. Cheers to this year, and many, many more.

To my in-laws, your love and support mean the world to me. Thank you for being such a great example of amazing educators, wonderful parents, and a loving couple. I could not ask for better in-laws or grandparents for my children. Also, thank you for encouraging me to be an educator myself.

To all of my past teachers, I appreciate you from the bottom of my heart. Thank you for always making me feel welcome, always encouraging my love for writing, and for the impact that you made in my life.

To my master teacher, Kay Williams Pierce, thank you for being the master teacher I needed. To this day, your insight and wisdom inspire me. I am so thankful we have had this opportunity to work alongside each other at our current school.

To my colleague, Stacey Roozeboom, you are amazing. Thank you for your time and energy reading over parts of the manuscript during the initial drafting phase. Your friendship means the world to me.

To my teacher besties, Jenna, Caitlin, Katie, Amber, Stacey, and Jessica, you make going to work enjoyable. I cherish our lunches together, but even more so, I am happy to have you all as friends.

About the Author

Christina is a high school English and journalism teacher in Southern California. She is a first-generation college graduate, receiving a degree in journalism and political science from the University of Nevada, and she earned her Master of Education and single-subject teaching credential in English from the University of La Verne. She is passionate about creating engaging, hands-on, and relatable lessons for her students, infusing writing instruction and instructional strategies together. She has presented multiple times at the California Association of English Teachers annual convention. You can find engaging instructional ideas and activities on her blog at thedaringenglishteacher.com and on Instagram at @thedaringenglishteacher.

References

Althoff, Sarah E., Kristen J. Linde, John D. Mason, Ninja M. Nagel, and Kathleen A. O'Reilly. 2007. "Posting and Communicating Daily Learning Objectives to Increase Student Achievement and Motivation." *Saint Xavier University & Pearson Achievement Solutions* (May): 58.

"Collaborative Learning/Learning with Peers | Writing." n.d. Dartmouth Writing Program. Accessed June 16, 2023. https://writing.dartmouth.edu/teaching/first-year-writing-pedagogies-methods-design/collaborative-learninglearning-peers.

Donnelly, Whitney B., and Christopher J. Row. 2010. "Using Sentence Frames to Develop Academic Vocabulary for English Learners." 2nd ed. *The Reading Teacher* 64. https://link.gale.com/apps/doc/A239813801/AONE?.

Fisher, Douglas, and Nancy Frey. 2013. "Gradual Release of Responsibility Instructional Framework." Keys to Literacy. https://keystoliteracy.com/wp-content/uploads/2017/08/2014. "Making the Most of Mentor Texts." ASCD. https://www.ascd.org/el/articles/making-the-most-of-mentor-texts.

Geigle, Bryce A. 2014. "How Color Coding Formulaic Writing Enhances Organization: A Qualitative Approach for Measuring Student Affect." https://files.eric.ed.gov/fulltext/ED554555.pdf.

Gibbons, Pauline. 2002. *Scaffolding Language, Scaffolding Learning: Teaching Second Language Learners in the Mainstream Classroom.* Portsmouth, NH: Heinemann.

References

Medina, Susan. 1994. *Teaching Academic Essay Writing: Accelerating the Process*. U.S. Department of Education. Accessed June 13, 2023. https://files.eric.ed.gov/fulltext/ED417412.pdf.

Pearson, P. David, and Margaret C. Gallagher. 1983. "The Instruction of Reading Comprehension." *Contemporary Educational Psychology* 8, no. 3 (July): 317–344.

Wiggins, Grant P., and Jay McTighe. 2005. *Understanding by Design*. Alexandria, Va.: Association for Supervision and Curriculum Development.

More from Dave Burgess Consulting, Inc.

Since 2012, DBCI has published books that inspire and equip educators to be their best. For more information on our titles or to purchase bulk orders for your school, district, or book study, visit DaveBurgessConsulting.com/DBCIbooks.

The Like a PIRATE™ Series
Teach Like a PIRATE by Dave Burgess
eXPlore Like a PIRATE by Michael Matera
Learn Like a PIRATE by Paul Solarz
Plan Like a PIRATE by Dawn M. Harris
Play Like a PIRATE by Quinn Rollins
Run Like a PIRATE by Adam Welcome
Tech Like a PIRATE by Matt Miller

The Lead Like a PIRATE™ Series
Lead Like a PIRATE by Shelley Burgess and Beth Houf
Balance Like a PIRATE by Jessica Cabeen, Jessica Johnson, and Sarah Johnson
Lead beyond Your Title by Nili Bartley
Lead with Appreciation by Amber Teamann and Melinda Miller
Lead with Collaboration by Allyson Apsey and Jessica Gomez
Lead with Culture by Jay Billy
Lead with Instructional Rounds by Vicki Wilson

Lead with Literacy by Mandy Ellis
She Leads by Dr. Rachael George and Majalise W. Tolan

The EduProtocol Field Guide Series
Deploying EduProtocols by Kim Voge, with Jon Corippo and Marlena Hebern
The EduProtocol Field Guide by Marlena Hebern and Jon Corippo
The EduProtocol Field Guide: Book 2 by Marlena Hebern and Jon Corippo
The EduProtocol Field Guide: Math Edition by Lisa Nowakowski and Jeremiah Ruesch
The EduProtocol Field Guide: Primary Edition by Benjamin Cogswell and Jennifer Dean
The EduProtocol Field Guide: Social Studies Edition by Dr. Scott M. Petri and Adam Moler

Leadership & School Culture
Beyond the Surface of Restorative Practices by Marisol Rerucha
Change the Narrative by Henry J. Turner and Kathy Lopes
Choosing to See by Pamela Seda and Kyndall Brown
Culturize by Jimmy Casas
Discipline Win by Andy Jacks
Educate Me! by Dr. Shree Walker with Micheal D. Ison
Escaping the School Leader's Dunk Tank by Rebecca Coda and Rick Jetter
Fight Song by Kim Bearden
From Teacher to Leader by Starr Sackstein
If the Dance Floor Is Empty, Change the Song by Joe Clark
The Innovator's Mindset by George Couros
It's OK to Say "They" by Christy Whittlesey
Kids Deserve It! by Todd Nesloney and Adam Welcome
Leading the Whole Teacher by Allyson Apsey
Let Them Speak by Rebecca Coda and Rick Jetter
The Limitless School by Abe Hege and Adam Dovico
Live Your Excellence by Jimmy Casas

Next-Level Teaching by Jonathan Alsheimer
The Pepper Effect by Sean Gaillard
Principaled by Kate Barker, Kourtney Ferrua, and Rachael George
The Principled Principal by Jeffrey Zoul and Anthony McConnell
Relentless by Hamish Brewer
The Secret Solution by Todd Whitaker, Sam Miller, and Ryan Donlan
Start. Right. Now. by Todd Whitaker, Jeffrey Zoul, and Jimmy Casas
Stop. Right. Now. by Jimmy Casas and Jeffrey Zoul
Teach Your Class Off by CJ Reynolds
Teachers Deserve It by Rae Hughart and Adam Welcome
They Call Me "Mr. De" by Frank DeAngelis
Thrive through the Five by Jill M. Siler
Unmapped Potential by Julie Hasson and Missy Lennard
When Kids Lead by Todd Nesloney and Adam Dovico
Word Shift by Joy Kirr
Your School Rocks by Ryan McLane and Eric Lowe

Technology & Tools
50 Things to Go Further with Google Classroom by Alice Keeler and Libbi Miller
50 Things You Can Do with Google Classroom by Alice Keeler and Libbi Miller
50 Ways to Engage Students with Google Apps by Alice Keeler and Heather Lyon
140 Twitter Tips for Educators by Brad Currie, Billy Krakower, and Scott Rocco
Block Breaker by Brian Aspinall
Building Blocks for Tiny Techies by Jamila "Mia" Leonard
Code Breaker by Brian Aspinall
The Complete EdTech Coach by Katherine Goyette and Adam Juarez
Control Alt Achieve by Eric Curts
The Esports Education Playbook by Chris Aviles, Steve Isaacs, Christine Lion-Bailey, and Jesse Lubinsky
Google Apps for Littles by Christine Pinto and Alice Keeler
Master the Media by Julie Smith

Raising Digital Leaders by Jennifer Casa-Todd
Reality Bytes by Christine Lion-Bailey, Jesse Lubinsky, and Micah Shippee, PhD
Sail the 7 Cs with Microsoft Education by Becky Keene and Kathi Kersznowski
Shake Up Learning by Kasey Bell
Social LEADia by Jennifer Casa-Todd
Stepping Up to Google Classroom by Alice Keeler and Kimberly Mattina
Teaching Math with Google Apps by Alice Keeler and Diana Herrington
Teaching with Google Jamboard by Alice Keeler and Kimberly Mattina
Teachingland by Amanda Fox and Mary Ellen Weeks

Teaching Methods & Materials
All 4s and 5s by Andrew Sharos
Boredom Busters by Katie Powell
The Classroom Chef by John Stevens and Matt Vaudrey
The Collaborative Classroom by Trevor Muir
Copyrighteous by Diana Gill
CREATE by Bethany J. Petty
Ditch That Homework by Matt Miller and Alice Keeler
Ditch That Textbook by Matt Miller
Don't Ditch That Tech by Matt Miller, Nate Ridgway, and Angelia Ridgway
EDrenaline Rush by John Meehan
Educated by Design by Michael Cohen, The Tech Rabbi
Empowered to Choose: A Practical Guide to Personalized Learning by Andrew Easton
Expedition Science by Becky Schnekser
Frustration Busters by Katie Powell
Fully Engaged by Michael Matera and John Meehan
Game On? Brain On! by Lindsay Portnoy, PhD
Guided Math AMPED by Reagan Tunstall

Happy & Resilient by Roni Habib
Innovating Play by Jessica LaBar-Twomy and Christine Pinto
Instant Relevance by Denis Sheeran
Instructional Coaching Connection by Nathan Lang-Raad
Keeping the Wonder by Jenna Copper, Ashley Bible, Abby Gross, and Staci Lamb
LAUNCH by John Spencer and A.J. Juliani
Learning in the Zone by Dr. Sonny Magana
Lights, Cameras, TEACH! by Kevin J. Butler
Make Learning MAGICAL by Tisha Richmond
Pass the Baton by Kathryn Finch and Theresa Hoover
Project-Based Learning Anywhere by Lori Elliott
Pure Genius by Don Wettrick
The Revolution by Darren Ellwein and Derek McCoy
The Science Box by Kim Adsit and Adam Peterson
Shift This! by Joy Kirr
Skyrocket Your Teacher Coaching by Michael Cary Sonbert
Spark Learning by Ramsey Musallam
Sparks in the Dark by Travis Crowder and Todd Nesloney
Table Talk Math by John Stevens
Teachables by Cheryl Abla and Lisa Maxfield
Unpack Your Impact by Naomi O'Brien and LaNesha Tabb
The Wild Card by Hope and Wade King
Writefully Empowered by Jacob Chastain
The Writing on the Classroom Wall by Steve Wyborney
You Are Poetry by Mike Johnston
You'll Never Guess What I'm Saying by Naomi O'Brien
You'll Never Guess What I'm Thinking About by Naomi O'Brien

Inspiration, Professional Growth & Personal Development
Be REAL by Tara Martin
Be the One for Kids by Ryan Sheehy
The Coach ADVenture by Amy Illingworth
Creatively Productive by Lisa Johnson
The Ed Branding Book by Dr. Renae Bryant and Lynette White

More from Dave Burgess Consulting, Inc.

Educational Eye Exam by Alicia Ray
The EduNinja Mindset by Jennifer Burdis
Empower Our Girls by Lynmara Colón and Adam Welcome
Finding Lifelines by Andrew Grieve and Andrew Sharos
The Four O'Clock Faculty by Rich Czyz
How Much Water Do We Have? by Pete and Kris Nunweiler
P Is for Pirate by Dave and Shelley Burgess
A Passion for Kindness by Tamara Letter
The Path to Serendipity by Allyson Apsey
PheMOMenal Teacher by Annick Rauch
Recipes for Resilience by Robert A. Martinez
Rogue Leader by Rich Czyz
Sanctuaries by Dan Tricarico
Saving Sycamore by Molly B. Hudgens
The Secret Sauce by Rich Czyz
Shattering the Perfect Teacher Myth by Aaron Hogan
Stories from Webb by Todd Nesloney
Talk to Me by Kim Bearden
Teach Better by Chad Ostrowski, Tiffany Ott, Rae Hughart, and Jeff Gargas
Teach Me, Teacher by Jacob Chastain
Teach, Play, Learn! by Adam Peterson
The Teachers of Oz by Herbie Raad and Nathan Lang-Raad
TeamMakers by Laura Robb and Evan Robb
Through the Lens of Serendipity by Allyson Apsey
Write Here and Now by Dan Tricarico
The Zen Teacher by Dan Tricarico

Children's Books
The Adventures of Little Mickey by Mickey Smith Jr.
Alpert by LaNesha Tabb
Alpert & Friends by LaNesha Tabb
Beyond Us by Aaron Polansky
Cannonball In by Tara Martin
Dolphins in Trees by Aaron Polansky

Dragon Smart by Tisha and Tommy Richmond
I Can Achieve Anything by MoNique Waters
I Want to Be a Lot by Ashley Savage
The Magic of Wonder by Jenna Copper, Ashley Bible, Abby Gross, and Staci Lamb
Micah's Big Question by Naomi O'Brien
The Princes of Serendip by Allyson Apsey
Ride with Emilio by Richard Nares
A Teacher's Top Secret Confidential by LaNesha Tabb
A Teacher's Top Secret: Mission Accomplished by LaNesha Tabb
The Wild Card Kids by Hope and Wade King
Zom-Be a Design Thinker by Amanda Fox